From the Farm to the Cockpit
The Log of a B-24 Co-pilot

From the Farm to the Cockpit
Copyright ©2012 by Tom H. Pine
ISBN: 978-0-9843239-1-3

Original Log by Charles A. Haynes
Additional Text and Editing by T. H. Pine
Transcribing & Editing by Marilyn Pine

All rights reserved. No part of this book may be reproduced, stored in a retrieval system or transmitted in any form or by any means without the prior written permission of the publishers, except by a reviewer who may quote brief passages in a review to be printed in a newspaper, magazine or journal.

La Maison Publishing, Inc.

www.lamaisonpub.com

ISBN: 978-0-9843239-1-3

From the Farm to the Cockpit
The Log of a B-24 Co-pilot

*To those brave men, who faced, and face,
death in the skies on a daily basis ... we owe
you so much.*

Table of Contents

Introduction..5
Foreword..7
Log Introduction & Service Tablet Pages...................15
September – 1944...21
Photos...126
January – 1945...135

Introduction

I write fiction. So, what am I, a novelist, doing writing non-fiction? In the truest sense of the word, I didn't write the book you now hold in your hands; I *assembled* it and shepherded it through to publication.

This story, part of the human drama of World War II, began some seventy years ago, when a somewhat frightened young man of twenty, left his rural beginnings in West Virginia and had to face his possible end at the controls of a B-24 bomber in a land he had only read about in school.

As it happened, this particular young man also had a gift for writing and jotted down a daily chronicle of his time in Italy, flying missions into Germany; his part in the worldwide conflagration that swept up so many young lives like his. Though I'm sure he didn't think of it that way, he became the caretaker of a discrete portion of history, penned in his own hand; a history lovingly preserved by him and his son over the years.

Because of this, I had the privilege to become part of this human drama and organize it into this book. I've attempted to step aside as much as possible and let this brave man tell his own story—his way—so that you, the reader can, through the lens of his writing, look into the past, a past not so different from our own time.

Foreword

I've heard it said that WW II will provide fodder for stories for centuries and, true to that thought, just when you think you've seen, read, or heard about all there is to tell about that war, something new crops up. This book contains a log, kept by a young pilot raised in West Virginia, who, faced with fighting in a world war far from his home, decided to put his thoughts on paper. What you will read is a very personal, individual chronicle of one young man's experience; an experience he had the perspicacity to enshrine in history.

The B-24 "Liberator" bomber, also known by the sobriquet, "The Flying Boxcar," because of its slab-sided construction, proved to be one of the workhorses of WW II, especially in the European Theater of the war. Built under contract with Consolidated Aircraft of San Diego, California,

America produced more Liberators than any other combat aircraft of WW II. Incorporating many advances in design, it holds the distinction of being the first bomber to employ "tricycle landing gear," which kept the plane level with the ground, unlike the previous "tail-draggers," which elevated the cockpit and hindered forward visibility while taxiing.

The rugged B-17 remained more popular with aircrews, however, due to the B-24 bomber's vulnerability to battle damage. The placement of its fuel tanks in the upper fuselage, coupled to its lightweight construction, gave it a tendency to catch fire. Nevertheless, it provided excellent service in a variety of roles, due to its heavy bomb carrying capacity, long range (2,100-3,700 miles), relatively fast cruising speed (215 mph) and high service ceiling (28,000 feet).

B-24 bombers had crews of seven to ten men, who manned machine guns positioned in the nose, tail, belly and sides of the aircraft. These highly motivated machine gunners, with their heavy, .50 caliber machine guns, gave the large aircraft a sting, as many an enemy fighter pilot discovered to his detriment.

Most people today have little to no idea what the pilots and crews of B-24 bombers endured. Explosions on takeoff, failure of one or more of its four, radial engines in flight, damage from flak (read a description of flak on pg. 233) and enemy fighters made daily life for a bomber pilot a horror. Often, execrable living conditions and extremes of weather made life at their home bases less than idyllic, to be sure.

Since B-24 raids utilized mass formations of these aircraft, battle damage proved severe and crews suffered greatly at the hands of fighter pilots and antiaircraft batteries. The heavy bomb load made control in formation flying a problem and damaged planes would often collide with undamaged planes in the tight formations. The psychological strain of seeing friends lost in combat due to flak and fighter plane incursions, coupled to the high attrition rate on any given mission, took its toll on morale, to say the least.

Interminable down time, with little to do due to bad weather, maintenance delays and called-off missions, frustrated crews used to the intensity of combat. The absence of a social life and delayed mail from home added to the strain.

In the event an aircraft went down, due to damage that made it impossible to sustain flight, crews that managed to "hit the silk" and parachute from it before it crashed had to endure the rigors and deprivations of the return to base. Add to this the possibility of injuries to a crewmember in the descent and a successful return could prove miraculous. Return trips, often through hostile territory, would not be possible without the help of partisans on the ground.

All of the above made the words, "He was a bomber pilot in World War II," the understatement of the twentieth century. The romance of the fighter pilot, going one-on-one with the enemy, overshadows the special brand of courage required to pilot a B-24, or any other heavy bomber.

Fighter pilots considered the bomber pilots "truck drivers" and imagined themselves as the gallant air-cavalry, riding to the aid of the lumbering bomb-droppers. Keep in mind that long-range bombers left fighter protection far behind on a mission (not until the advent of the P-51 fighter plane, late in the war, were fighters able to stay with a bomber formation over the target) and, once at their targets, bombers had to rely on their on-board 50-caliber machine guns to survive.

What you are about to read and experience is the personal log of Lieutenant Charles A. Haynes, a B-

24 co-pilot, who preferred the nickname Chuck. He writes, "I, the co-pilot, decided that before I went to sleep that night I would jot down a few notes relative to the day's happenings. My diary is the result—certainly no literary work—just the daily musings of a scared kid forced by circumstances into a man's job."

Using "Service Tablets," Chuck proceeded aptly to describe the feelings he experienced when faced with his own mortality. "One thing I've noticed is how one gets accustomed to the idea of dying, of the approach of the possibility of death. I, of course, think no desire or urge will ever come before the desire of self-preservation, but I do know that as time goes by that desire becomes somewhat numb or deadened, at least less acute, as one becomes accustomed to the presence of the possibility." On page after page of neatly written script, Chuck filled those tablets with a personal narrative that provides more than just a history of WW II; one man's personal journey through a time few of us can imagine, no less experience.

That Chuck survived to pass this diary on to us is, in itself, testament to the hand of Providence. As you read his narrative, day by day, from September 1944 to June 1945, you will experience the boredom, fear, longing and, yes, *humor* of one man's view of a conflict that ravaged the world in the middle of the Twentieth Century.

Chuck proved an adept writer, capable of infusing what would normally be a routine recitation of facts with the emotion he felt at the time. Despite his humble description, this diary IS a literary work in its own right, a human story of a distinct part of history, written, not by a professional military man, but by a young *American* man, snatched from his home on the farm and thrust onto the world stage. His courage and determination stands as testament to the human spirit of the often snidely referred-to "common man" and what he is capable of when called upon to serve his country and the cause of freedom.

As you read, you will experience, not the scribings of an historian writing after the fact, but the immediate, *personal* recollection of one man, now gone to be with his ancestors, who joined millions in a conflict that has provided untold reams of historical and fictitious literature, films, and psychological insight into the horrors of war.

[NOTE ON LOG ENTRIES: Taken verbatim from the original, handwritten log, provided by Charles's son, David Haynes, these are not the polished writings of a scholar, but of a farm boy turned aviator, barely out of high school. I left he incorrect spelling, lack of punctuation, paragraph breaks and other anomalies as found in an effort to preserve the authenticity and integrity of this historical document and accurately reflect what the author had in his mind nearly seventy years ago when he penned the words—a *living chronicle*, worthy of preservation, left as is as much as possible. Any changes that exist are there solely for clarity. I take full responsibility for any errors. – T. H. Pine]

THE LOG OF A B-24 CO-PILOT
WWII, 15th Air Force, Italy

Detailed descriptions of events occurring during two Atlantic crossings and a tour of combat duty.

Combat includes "bail outs" of all ten crewmembers and on another occasion the landing of a badly damaged bomber on a fighter strip in Hungary.

This entire log is quoted directly from the personal diary of Lt. Charles A. Haynes, Co-Pilot of the crew of Lt. Curtis I. Eatman.

Lt. Eatman's crew was attached to the 782nd Squadron, 465th Bomb Group, 15th Air Force at Pantinella [Pantanella] Air Base, Foggia, Italy from Sept. 1944 to June 1945.

[Note: The Following are facsimiles of the actual handwritten pages from Charles Haynes log, which he wrote on pages of service tablets. – T. H. Pine]

16 Sept 1944

Flew from Topeka, Kansas to Grenier Field, Manchester, New Hampshire via St Louis, Toledo, Buffalo, etc. Was a very plesant trip. Flew over Lake Erie.

Had a quick processing line to go thru at Grenier and had to remain on the post.

17 Sept 1944

Left Grenier and flew to Gander Field, New Foundland. Was late getting off because we had to get a prop governor major changed.

The trip from Grenier to

Gander was very interesting. It may be the last we'll see of the U.S. for a long time. The flight over the St Lawrence and another large body of water was the longest over water flight we've made. Some of the boys put on their "mae wests."

Some of this country is such that you can't tell whether you are over water with lots of islands or over land with lots of lakes.

Haynes/Pine

HEADQUARTERS
DAVIS-MONTHAN FIELD AFB

SPECIAL ORDERS)   R-E-S-T-R-I-C-T-E-D
:
NUMBER……..236)   E X T R A C T

1. The Heavy Bombardment Combat Crews consisting of the military personnel listed on the atchd Incl #1, which is hereby made a part of this order, reld fr atchd-unasgd 233rd AAFBU RCC (H) (In Tng), Class TU 9-3, asgd Sec K, 272nd AAFBU (SB), AAB, Topeks, Kans, <u>WP 27 August 1944</u>, so as to arrive and report to CO not later than <u>5 Sept 1944</u>. EDC on H/R 3 Sept 44

Eight (8) days delay enroute, plus two (2) days travel time auth, but in no event will personnel report to new sta later than <u>5 Sept 1944.</u>

This is a <u>temporary</u> change of sta Trav being of temp nature, That govt expense of dependents and household good not auth, except as provided for in AR 55-120. Qrs asgmt of 0 terminated effective date of departure in accordance with AR 210-10, Par 13.

No per diem at TAAB, Topeka, Kans auth. Payment of mileage not auth. Prov of pars 5 and 6, WD 260, dd 26 June 44, will apply. TOT if desired.

<u>For 0:</u> 0 will be reimbursed for actual cost of rail transportation fr this sta to Topeka, Kans if govt T/R is not furn.

<u>For EM:</u> IGF rations in kind fr this sta to Topeka, Kns while trav, FD pay in advance monetary alws in lieu thereof as prescribed in Sec II, AR 35-45620 for ea EM for two (2) days ea. Under prov of AR 35-4540, as amended, EM auth an alws of three (3) cents per rile for trav fr this sta to destination where govt T/R is not furn. EM last rationed this sta to include supper, 26 August 1944.

TO auth to ship personal effects of personnel to AAB, Topeka, Kans.
TDN: 501-25 P 432-02-03-07-08 A 212/50425. Auth: TWX IIAF EM 4446, dd 20 Aug 1944 and IIAF Memo 35-2, dd 11 Apr 1944.

By order of Colonel RICH:

STUART G. CROSS
OFFICIAL: Capt AC
    DAVID H. DOTSON   Adj
    1st Lt AC

Asst Adj

Crew #6389
2D LT (1092) EATMAN, CURTIS I., 0 825 130 (P)
2D LT (1051) HAYNES, CHARLES A., 0 828 426 (CP)
FLT O (1034) EVANS, WILLIAM E, JR, T 127 579 (N)
2D LT (1035) MAGEE, WILLIAM T., JR, 0 777 009 (B)
CPL (757) POWELL, JAMES P., 18 137 902 (ROG)
SGT (748) PAKES, LAMOND H., 16 150 919 (EG)
CPL (612) WANSER, HAROLD J., 35 029 837 (AG)
SGT (611) DEARMAN, JOE R., 14 152 543 (CG)
CPL (611) HAHN, EDWARD W., JR, 19 141 106 (CG)
T SGT (611) JAY, ANDREW, JR, 14 055 424 (CG)

September 1944

16 Sept 1944

Flew from Topeka, Kansas to Grenier Field, Manchester, New Hampshire via St. Louis, Toledo, Buffalo, etc. Was a very pleasant trip. Flew over Lake Erie.

Had a quick processing line to go thru at Grenier and had to remain on the post

17 Sept 1944

Left Grenier and flew to Gander Field, Newfoundland. Was late getting off because we had to get a prop governor motor changed.

The trip from Grenier to Gander was very interesting. It may be the last we will see of the U.S. for a long time. The flight over the St. Lawrence and another large body of water was the longest over water flight we have made. Some of the boys put on their "Mae Wests."

Some of this country is such that you can't tell whether you are over water with lots of islands or over land with lots of lakes.

<u>18 Sept 1944</u>

Just laid around today. Started to take an engineering officer for a ride to check on our engines because they are overheating but the weather closed in before we got off. The weather here is very cold compared to Topeka or Manchester. We were uncomfortably cold with two blankets last nite. Saw a show at the post theater tonite.

<u>19 Sept 1944</u>

Took the engineering officer up this morning. Seems our main trouble is with our weight and balance. The ship does well when we get everything and every one well forward. We did get him to check on an oil leak in no 3 and think we will get some action on that.

It was a good ride and I enjoyed looking the country over again. Cy got called down from the tower for landing like a P-38. I thought it was a good landing.

Went to the show again tonite.

The only girls within hundreds of miles of here are about 400 Canadian W. D.'s stationed here and a few civilians, who work in PX etc. They are all easy marks but all are always pretty busy.

I get a kick out of the Newfoundland civilians here (men). They wear caps like they did in 1926 in US.

19 Sept 1944

Lots of the boys moved out today, but they're still working on our ship so we weren't alerted. Just played around. Slept late this morning, read and saw another show tonite.

20 Sept 1944

Slept late this morning. Went down to a nearby lake with Cy, Maggie, Jay, and Harry. I bumed a ride in a sailboat from a guy who has a camp here while the other boys rented a boat and fished. They didn't catch anything.

We wanted to take our new 45 cal pistols and test fire them but the MP's wouldn't let us off the field with them.

We went to see Micky Rooney in Girl Crazy but I didn't like it and left early.

We're alerted to leave tomorrow morn early.

21 Sept 1944 – Gander New Foundland

Had briefing and got all ready for flight to Azores at 1:00 this morning then had flight called off at last minute.

Slept most of the day. Spent a couple of hours in the post library.

I've already seen the show "Dragon Seed" back in the States.

22 Sept 44

Nothing today. Weather socked in.

23 Sept 1944

Had a big day today. Turned lights out to go to sleep at 12:30 and were called out to brief at 02:00. We left Gander field early this morning and flew across the north Atlantic to the Azores. Are now at Lagens Field. The flight took 7 ½ hours and is 1330 miles long. We still have a lot of water to fly over tomorrow.

This is a hell of a post. It's very dirty and dusty and there's nothing very desirable here.

The most impressive thing I have seen since I left the states is the quaint people, town, and landscape. The people go bare footed almost 100% tho I'm now in bed with two blankets over me. They either drive teams of oxen before two wheel ox carts or carry two buckets or baskets attached to the ends of a long springy pole over their shoulder. They walk with a springy step that seems to make the pole bend and bounce the load along.

Between the runways and everywhere there isn't army barracks etc there are funny looking houses and out buildings of the natives. Their fields are divided into plots no larger than a good sized living room and each one is surrounded by a high stone fence. The fences run every way and are very crooked and irregular. They are constructed of grey, round field stone and bound by some kind of grey mortar. It seems impossible that so much stone could have come from the land it surrounds.

I'll be glad to leave here, but I wouldn't have wanted to miss seeing the place for anything.

9-24-44 – Lagens Field Azores

We've been out of the US one week today. Guess this is my first Sunday overseas. We were quite surprised to wake up at about 10 00 this morning. We were to be woke up at 500 for briefing. Guess the weather was too bad.

I read a book, Steinbeck's "The Moon is Down," today and slept. The post theater is an open air affair and it's raining tonite. Some of the boys are at the show anyway.

Oh yes, I took a walk with Magee this afternoon. These quaint houses seem to not only house people but oxen, pigs, & chickens also.

9-25-44 – Merriketch [Marrakech] French Moroco

Had a very nice ride from the Azores here. The navigator was on the ball for a change. We're quartered in a large, masonry house that was formerly the home of a wealthy family.

The post is ok, but not as much as we've been accustomed to in the states. Candy, cigarettes etc are rationed. The franc is used 100% here. One franc is worth 2¢.

They have characters who I presume are deasert Arabs here to do the work on the post. It's quite odd to see a bunch of old men like you see in the movies with long black or white robes, turbans, sandles or bare footed, and a pipe with a stem a couple feet long in a case strapped over their shoulder, sweeping off the apron or taxi way.

The part of Africa over which we flew was desert as one would imagine but much more thickly inhabited than I had thought it would be. What looked like corals and buildings could be seen about every mile in all directions. Not at all like the vast uninhabited areas of our own mid west.

Guess I'll maybe see a different type of land in a day or so when we go north east to Tunis.

<u>9-26-44 – Merriketch [Marrakech]</u>

Nothing new today. We just slept and laid around. Hope for a briefing and flight out of here tomorrow.

9-27-44 –Tunis, Tunisia

Left Moroco about 9 this morning and got in here at 2:30. About half the flight was above the overcast. This is a large base and there is lots of equipment here both US, British, and a lot of captured Italian and German stuff.

Italian prisoners do the barracks orderly, truck driving and construction details. They are very happy about their present condition.

There is a lot of construction going on here, tho they say the place is still very heavily mined. We're cautioned not to touch anything that looks suspicious.

The barracks are big white three story masonry buildings that were used by the Germans. They are very poorly equipped as far as toilet facilities go.

This is the first place we have been where there is real evidence of war. Lots of the buildings have been shelled and are only partly or sometimes completely destroyed.

I went to the show tonite in a theater that only had the stage and a small portion of the roof left, the rest having been bombed away. I sat way up high on a scaffold which they're using to reconstruct the building.

The beds are better here. We have cotton mattresses instead of the straw we had at Merriketch [Marrakech].

The food is very good and unbelievably cheap. A meal cost 5 francs, or 10¢.

9-28-44 – Tunis

I managed to get a pass for Cy and myself today and we went to town. It was very interesting but parts of it were also quite repulsive.

The market place is under the town, you might say, in the sewers; but that would hardly be correct either because there are no sewers as such. The refuse and debris which naturally collects from human existence is everywhere.

The merchants ask unreasonable prices for their wares, but will also pay fabulous sums for ordinary U. S. articles. A 10¢ package of cigarettes can easily be sold for $1.00, .40¢ for a stick of gum and $5.00 for 10¢ store lipstick. Unfortunately, I left all my lipstick in the U.S.

We saw the king's palace. The throne room, private quarters and harem rooms were very expensively decorated but weren't too practical, it appeared to me. The guide made a point of telling the prices of everything. Two very ordinary looking gold clocks, except for dirty tarnished gold frames that held them, placed on each side of the king's bed were supposed to have cost one million dollars each, or that is the equivalent of that in francs.

There are some French and Jewish women here that don't look too repulsive to boys who have been out of the country for a while. There is, however, a price on everything. All the kids on the streets are looking for business for their big sisters. They have no hesitancy what so ever of approaching one with the most vulgar and obscene language. Their propositions are always very direct and to the point.

There is an officers club in the best hotel where one can lounge around, drink at the bar, if hes so inclined, as most everyone is, or get a good meal for 5 francs (10¢). We are cautioned to eat no where else in town as lots of disease prevails here.

Travel in town is mostly by streetcar tho you see a few private motor vehicles and as many horse-drawn conveyances. Some of the street cars very much resemble the "Toonerville Troley" of U. S. comic strips. They were obviously built for 4 or 5 passengers and now operate with 30 or 40 in and hanging all over it. Others are open affairs with only the seats and a top, no windows, or maybe I should say "all windows." They run them very slowly, three or four hooked together, and make very few stops. You just run like hell and grab the thing and jump on, and can expect to see an old Arab in a sheet and turban, who is the conductor , come running thru the crowd of standing passengers to collect your fare, which is almost nothing. Never more than 1 ½ francs (3¢).

9-29-44

Spent ½ day in the sack and the other half in town. Had a good time in town.

9-30-44

Same as above, only had a better time in town. My date is beginning to learn English and I French. That's "bon."

October 1944

10-1-44 – San Pancrozio Airdome, Italy

Had a bunch of messy weather enroute Tunis to Gioie. We couldn't get thru to Gioie so we flew thru a lot of weather at 1000' over the water to here as an alternate.

The runway is o.k. but the field is soft mud. Billeting facilities are very limited. We're sleeping in the infirmary. Food not bad.

10-2-44

Just loafed around the infirmary all morning and went into Leece in the afternoon Leece is no good. Streets are so narrow pedestrians duck into doors while GI trucks go by. Was impressed by the extensive vineyards. They grow grapes like they do cotton in alabama.

10-3-44 – Gioia, Italy

Slept all morning and played poker till 300 PM then flew to Gioia.

Its very poor here. We live in tents and eat out of mess kits in a filthy tent mess hall. Washing and toilet facilities are terrible.

Food is bad. We're eating mostly K rations.

10-4-33

Slept all day and wrote a few letters. Got my first mail today. Had a letter from Louise 9-15-44, and one from Mother, also one "v mail" from Aunt Clo.

10-5-44

Slept all morning. Wrote, read, and played poker in the afternoon and went to town and saw a show tonite. Finished the day with more poker. It rained and been muddy and disagreeable since we've been here.

10-6-44

Rested all day.

10-7-44

Same.

10-8-44 – Pantenella [sic Pantanella]

Trucks came for us at noon. We loaded the truck and trailer at the ship and kissed it goodbye. Left Goioa [Gioia] at 300 PM and arrived here 6:30. Had a very pleasant ride and enjoyed the scenery. We stopped the truck once to cross a stone fence and get grapes.

Today was Sunday and all the little towns were simply packed full of men. The streets were joined from building to building. The driver would blow his horn and the wops would scatter enough for him to get by somehow.

They seemed to have just turned out to stand around and shoot the breeze.

The wop kids have learned to say "Hi Joe" and insisted on screaming that at us always.

10-9-44

Slept in the enlisted men's club last nite. They put us up a tent today. We have no floor and water is very scarce, tho we do have enough of that for necessities. They say they'll get us an electric light soon.

There is a pretty good officers club here and the food is good.

10-10-44

Had lectures on "Combat," Emergency Procedures," Escape" and such things in the morning. Also issued additional equipment and had some "brush up" lectures on "turrets."

This afternoon Maggie and Cy had a flight with the Major. They say they messed up pretty badly. Also Monty (engineer) wasn't too sharp. Couldn't find the fuel valves when they were right in front of him.

Rabbit and I enlarged our tent by raising the back up to form more top and filling in around the three exposed sides with shelter halves.

Had the usual medical lecture at 7:00 tonite.

We've been hearing a lot of bad rumors about combat. Guess its rough.

10-11-44

Checked in and out with Personnel Equipment today, thats all.

10-12-44

Cy had a mission as co-pilot today. Said it was an easy one. A little flak but not too bad. I had a stove made from an oil drum and put it up. The pipe is empty shell cans.

10-13-44

Friday 13 today. Cy flew another ride as co-pilot. Went up in central Germany. Said it was plenty rough. We're all pretty dejected tonite. A plane went down in flames right beside him. He says the flak is terrible. We figure 5% is a good figure for looses. That means in 20 missions it should be us.

We spent some of the evening getting our equipment ready for tomorrow, but an orderly just came in and said we had been scratched. We all heaved a sigh of relief and are now ready to turn in. Lots of replacements came in tonite. About all of the empty tents have been filled. They are a noisy bunch, but will quiet down when they learn the score here, as we did.

10-14-44

Went to the line today and exchanged our chest chutes for backpacks. I don't think there will be much time to put on a chest pack when the time comes to use it.

Read and slept the rest of day.

10-15-44

Sunday – Went to church in the morning and wrote letters in the afternoon.

10-16-44

Didn't have to fly again today. Built a frame around the inside of the tent and extended the back. Also built a door and some shelves. It's much better now.

We're scheduled to fly tomorrow.

10-17-44

Big day today. Our first mission and it was a mean one. We did get double credit for it, tho. Bombed a target in Vienna. The sky was black with flak and I don't see how anyone kept from getting knocked down. Going through that stuff is really horrible. You can only sit there and watch it. The black puffs look harmless but when you see a few planes go down in flames around you you certainly develope a fear of them.

The formation went all to pieces over the target. Planes turned off every way. I guess there were about 100 planes in our so called formation. I saw only one fighter and he made a pass at a B24 stragler and the tail gunner shot him down. He just exploded and broke into three flaming pieces.

We got one hole in the nose turret and a crack in my windshield. It was just a little piece that hit my glass, but it did knock slivers against my goggles.

The list for tomorrow is not up yet. The weather wasn't good today and I think it wioll be worse tomorrow. We went through lots of clouds today which isn't good in any formation.

I'm damn tired tonite.

10-18-44

We were scheduled to fly today but were scratched late last nite. Just laid around all day and went to the show tonite.

10-19-44

Had a standown today no one flew. Just laid around again and listened to the rain on the top of the tent.

10-20-44

Had a lovely mission today. Was up to Munic and did not have a target in the flak area. Saw no fighters either. The only casualties were two ships that colided in the formation. One cut the others tail off and the one sans tail fell end over end into the Adriatic Ocean from 17000 feet. Only two chutes came out. It was quite gruesome. The other ship flew back home.

There were lots of clouds at the target and the radar man wasn't on the ball. We saw the bombs hit in an open field. That was disgusting too.

Don't have to fly tomorrow.

Oh yes, we crossed the Alps today twice. They look just like I've always imagined they would only with a little more snow. The whole mass of mountains are covered with snow instead of just the tops as I had supposed. To look down on all that snow made the low temperature in the ship seem even colder.

The land between the Adriatic and the Alps in Italy really looks like good flat country. Reminded me of some of the better parts of California.

10-21-44

Nothing today. Slept and read.

10-22-44

Same.

10-23-44

Started on a mission to northern Italy. Climbed with formation to 2300 feet up over the Adriatic but couldn't get above the clouds. Got about half way up the boot and returned.

I landed the ship, at the direction of the tower, down wind, with the bomb load, and nearly failed to stop at the end of the runway. It was too close for comfort. It'll make me more careful next time.

10-24-44

Slept, read & wrote letters.

10-25-44

We spent most of the day after we got up getting a stove pipe fixed up. Secured the use of an ox-aceline welding outfit and made a 7 inch pipe out of centers of insulated wine spools. Had to cut the flanged ends off and then spot weld them together.

Maggie and Hahn, who've said all along that they could weld, couldn't do a bit of good with the torch. We finally got Monty and he's good. Can make as good a bead as I ever saw.

The stove is very satisfactory now.

Had one of the boys who was going to Bari pick up our mail. We all got some which made us quite happy.

I heard from home as of Oct 13&14. Had three letters from Jeanne & 3 from Jo Gibson.

<u>10-26-44</u>

Built a floor in the tent today out of packing boxes. We're only about half thru tonite. It turned out to be quite a job with no tools (one small ballpean hammer and a crash axe and a pair of pliers) and the ground in here is quite irregular.

The officers are having a party tonite. Are supposed to have in about 20 nurses from surrounding hospitals. There are only about 100 officers here in the squadron so I don't plan much fun. May go over and listen to the music. Guess it will be pretty drunk over there.

10-27-44

Finished putting floor in tent and built two chairs.

10-28-44

We're briefed for a very rough mission. One of Herman's pet industries a long way into Germany. Were told we'd no doubt get fighters.

No need to say we were indeed glad when it was called off due to bad weather.

10-29-44

This is the first Sunday I've had to fly since I've been here. We had a General with the formation today. Had started for a production plant at Prague but the weather stopped us just before landfall over the northern Adriatic. Circled there for an hour trying to get the formation above the clouds.

It's good we did not get over cause we lost two superchargers on the way back and were using much too much gas. I doubt that we could have gotten back across the Alps.

Went to church tonite. Church here is a routine. Every service is the same. We take communion every time.

Also along the line of sameness, the chaplin says the same prayer after every briefing before the missions. One can't help memorizing it.

We are very glad we aren't scheduled to fly tomorrows mission. Will sleep much better tonite (later too).

<u>10-30-44</u>

Nothing today.

<u>10-31-44</u>

Pay Day. I drew $500.00 for two months. Paid Cy the 100 I borrowed from him in Tucson when my wallet was stolen, and sent $300 home.

November 1944

11-1-44

I laid around and read all day. Cy & Maggie went to Bari. They got lots of old mail, a 100 watt bulb from the black market (cost $3.00) and several other things we needed.

11-2-44

Were briefed to Bleckhheimmer [sic Blechhammer] today. Were plenty glad when the mission was recalled because of weather. That's our roughest target. Its farther, has more flak, and chance of fighter interception than the others. There are several others that are considered just as bad, but we always dread that one for some reason. Wish the Russians would hurry and get it.

We went to the show tonite and saw "Three Jills and a Jeep." Was better than not going.

11-3-44

Had a practice mission scheduled for today, but it was called off because of weather also. I wouldn't have minded going on it. it would at least have been something to do.

Under these conditions one does a lot of thinking he would not ordinarily do. He also attaches a lot of significance to such things as shows, radio programs, letters from mild acquaintances, etc; such things as he would ordinarily consider trivial.

I think if I get back from here some of the thinking and reading that I would ordinarily not have had time to do will be beneficial to me.

One thing I've noticed is how one gets accustomed to the idea of dying, or the approach of the possibility of death. I, of course, think no desire or urge will ever come before the desire of self preservation. But I do know that as time goes by that desire becomes somewhat numb or deadened, at least less acute, as one becomes accustomed to the presence of the possibility.

I know that 5 or 6 months ago when I saw a sign by our orderly room in Lincoln Neb. reading "Combat Crew Headquarters" I was very startled and found it a bit hard to realize that I was on a combat crew and faced the possibility, slight though it seemed at the time, of meeting the enemy and then the even lesser possibility of dying. Gradually, however, as training continued and we learned bombing, evasive action etc, and I became used to seeing the word "combat" I lost my fear of it and accepted it just like my name or any other common word.

There were times later during the training and the flight across that the idea of death and the natural fear of it came to me but there was no other great surge of emotion until I actually reached the combat area.

I think that after the first shock; and I can call it that because I was shocked as the sight of the sign brought the realization of my situation forceably to my attention; the rate of the approach of combat did not exceed the rate at which my mind could become accustomed to its presence.

When I arrived here, however, and became acquainted with the circumstances; saw the empty tents with the number of missions by the doors, chalk marks, usually much less than fifty; saw crews I'd talked with the day before fail to return from missions; saw the ships full of patched flak holes, many in very vital spots; and heard the boys who had been here only a few weeks tell of the things they had seen on raids, I became obsessed with a very strong fear and found it very difficult to sleep at nights or to keep my thoughts out of letters home.

That fear did not have time to leave me before we got our first mission to Vienna and saw the flak come up in black puffs all about us. Saw other ships leave the formation with engines shot out and control surfaces shot away. Saw one ship just above us come down barely missing us with the whole right wing on fire. One ship way down in a lower box exploded leaving only a few pieces of burning debris floating downward.

There was no time to dwell on any of this. Just glance at it and before the significance of it had time to penetrate my already muddled mind my attention would be drawn to our own condition. The black puffs were all around ahead and behind. It looked like one should make an attempt to dodge the forward ones but on second thought it was better to stay with the formation as there was no way to predict where the next ones would burst.

After what seemed like eternity, but was only about 4 or 5 minutes we came out of the flak and there were no more black puffs. Our ship was ok as far as I could see except for a crack in my windshield (I about jumped out of my seat when the little piece of flak cracked it but immediately forgot it because of the other more momentous things happening) and an engine temperature gage that was out.

I slept very little that nite or the next four or five. In a few days we got another mission and because of weather didn't get over the target but bombed another where there was no flak.

I don't think it was so much that second mission as the time element that alleviated my dejection. Very gradually I've come to be at ease and reasonably happy. Now I can sleep o.k., even the nite before a mission waiting for the Sgt. to wake us up.

Sometimes now when I'm at briefing and they give us a very rough target I get a lump in my throat and a pretty acute pang of fear. The lump is also there when the chaplin says the prayer (he has a standard one hes memorized and never deviates from it) after each briefing. Generally, however, there is no fear and a very little bit of worry except at times when I just become dejected over minor things such as no mail or some little "run in" with one of the crew.

After a mission I always feel good. Its sorta like returning from a possible death and being given an assurance of life till the next one.

At first the periods of worry between missions would overlap. Now I never worry about a mission until at the earliest, the night before and usually not until briefing.

The United States seem to me like heaven. I mean that literly. I would ask for nothing more than to be there. I mean stationed there. Being a civilian or getting a leave, the things that were the ultimate when I was there, mean almost nothing now. Just to be there is all one wants.

If someone was going to give you a big Buick automobile and you could choose whether you wanted white sidewall tires or not you could liken the situation to the idea of going to the states and going home. If you could just go back it would be like getting the car. The business of the white sidewalls pretty much compares in importance as to having the choice of going back and remaining in the army or going back as a civilian.

The example is pretty crude, I know, but it may illustrate what I mean.

I'm just writing this stuff to pass the time anyway. Guess in the back of my head lies the idea that there is a possibility that I'll get to go home sometime and will get a kick out of reading it.

Was passing the orderly room today and got hooked for a co-pilot job for the Sqdn. Commander. He was flying a crew to Naples on their way to a rest camp at Capri.

We flew about half way to Naples and met a lot of weather. Were trying to get thru a pass in the mts and met clouds just rolling up the valleys at us.

After trying a couple of other passes and trying to go over it unsuccessfully we returned.

11-4-44

Had a mission to Linz, Germany today. The flak was pretty bad but not as bad as it was at Vienna. Had beautiful weather on the way but the target was covered with clouds. Had to bomb by radar and couldn't see the results.

Saw several German fighters and one jet propelled ship.

11-5-44

No mission for us today. Went to church this morning and read all afternoon and evening.

Have a mission scheduled for tomorrow.

11-6-44

Flew to Vienna today. But didn't drop any bombs. Someone who was leading the wing formation did not drop so no one else did. He said his radar equip didn't work.

We had good weather till we got to the target then it was a solid overcast below us. There was a wall of flak ahead but we missed it. I think that must have been the target. Dropped two booby trap bombs we were carrying in the Adriatic on the way back.

I think this mission was the hardest yet to me. We had a very bad ship. Lost one supercharger completely on the way up and partially lost two others. Had to pull between 45 & 50 inches of mercury most of the way to stay with the formation. That is that much on the engines we had left. No. 2 set on 30 inches all the time. I expected one of two of our remaining engines to go out any time.

11-7-44

We were scheduled to fly today, but someone found out it was an easy mission and scratched us to put on a crew that had 49 missions.

The crew that flew the ship we brought back yesterday lost an engine on takeoff (no. 3) but made it around the field somehow and landed.

I went to Spinizola this afternoon and picked up a few things we needed at the PX. It's only 20 miles, but it was a dirty, cold ride on the back of a truck. Don't think I'll go back soon.

11-8-44

We were scheduled to fly today but got a standown because of weather. Were then scheduled for a practice mission (of all things) here in the local area but were scratched from that due to lack of ships. That was a very good break. Those practice missions are a waste of gas, bombs, energy, and patience.

11-9-44

Cy and I went to Bari today and got our picture made. Had a pretty good time in town, but had a hell of a time getting back. Some jerk Britisher started us out on the wrong road. There are two roads out of Bari going north, a coastal route and an inland route. We got on the coastal route and were damn lucky to get back at all. Made it just in time for briefing this morning. Were about frozen. It was good the mission was called off.

11-10-44

Censored about 100 letters today and read. Thats all

11-11-44

Same.

11-12-44

Were briefed for a milk run to Brenner pass; did not get off because of weather.

11-13-44

Cy and I drew Highway Patrol detail for tonite. Went into Andria in a Jeep and met a British Nurse (captain) and were invited in for tea with her in the hospital. Spent the most enjoy able Evening since we arrived here.

11-14-44

Wrote, Read & slept all day. Got scratched from tomorrow's Mission because Maggie and Harry (ball turret Gunner) are on D. N. I. F.

11-15-44

Nothing today.

11-16-44

Taking life easy.

11-17-44

Big mission today. Bombed Vienna thru an undercast. The flak wasn't as bad as usual but still wasn't pleasant. Only four of the eight ships in our box got to the target. Seems everyone is scared of that one. Can't say that I blame them much. They find something wrong with the ship and chalk up an early return.

I'm damn tired and sleepy. Are up for another one tomorrow. We're expecting an easy one. Are carrying clusters.

11-18-44

Bombed a fighter field at Udine in north Italy with fragmentation clusters. Dropped 180-200 lb bombs from our ship alone. I'd certainly have hated to have been on or near that field.

We were supposed to get the parking area, but I think we covered most of north Italy. The fighters have been coming up from there and picking off stragglers and "early returns" from our formations.

We were also surprised at the amount of accurate flak they put up. Tho I didn't see any planes go down, I'm sure lots of them got flak holes.

We bombed from the funniest weather I've ever seen. At 22,000 feet there was a very large dark cloud over the target area that somewhat resembled smoke. You could see planes a couple of hundred yards away thru it but that's all. I was somewhat worried about a collision with another plane.

No mail tonite. I'm a bit dejected. Tried to read some of E. A. Poe tonite, but was disgusted with that.

11-19-44

Were scheduled for today, but they scratched us because of lack of ships. Went to church and laid around the rest of the day.

Are up for tomorrow.

11-20-44

Providence smiled on us today. Were briefed to hit the Blecheimmer [Blechhammer] south oil refinery. Its 700 miles there and is the toughest target in the whole 15th AF range. When we were about the middle of Yougoslavia, on the way up Hahn (Martin gunner) got sick, passed out twice, got abnormally red in the face, had a very high temp yet was freezing, and was shaking like he had the rickets. We called the box leader of the whole attack who in turn called the leader of the whole attack, who ordered us to bring him home.

Tonite the boys got back 1 hr late and were shot all to pieces. The man who sent us back had his ship exploded over the target. Lost four of the five ships that went over the target in that box. I sorta hated to be an early return, but I'm damn glad of it now.

Guess we'll fly again tomorrow.

Went to see Bing Crosby in "Going My Way" this afternoon. It was very good, tho I'd seen it in the States.

11-21-44

Nothing today.

11-22-44

Started to Munich today but had to keep climbing to stay above the overcast. Got as far as Salzburg, the alternate, and were at 28,000 ft. so we bombed it thru the overcast.

There wasn't much flak over the target, tho a couple of shells burst in our box. We had a good bit of flak on the way up. Got more in the north Italy than before.

We had an oxygen leak and had a rough time thinking about that. Just had enough to make it. If we'd have gone on to Munich, we couldn't have stayed at altitude.

Went to see the show tonite and saw "See Here, Pvt Hargrove."

11-23-44

Todays Thanksgiving. We had a standown because of bad weather. Had an intelligence lecture this morning and slept in the afternoon. Had turkey for dinner tonite.

11-24-44

Standown.

11-25-44

More of the same. I rode the mail truck to Spinizola, but found the PX closed for inventory as it seems it always is if you want something. Had a cup of coffee at the Red Cross and got a shave & much needed haircut.

11-26-44

Had an instrument calabration flight this afternoon. There were three ships going to the range at the same time so we flew formation at one to three hundred feet a hundred miles or so down to the southern cost of Italy. The calabration range is along the coast right in the arch of the foot of the boot. Rather enjoyed the trip. I gave my seat to Harry (ball gunner) and let him fly back.

11-27-44

Weather sacked in tight.

11-28-44

Same. Reading.

11-29-44

Ditto.

11-30-44

Same, except its payday. I sent mother $100 and a $25 $\underline{^{00}}$ bond and Peggy the same.

December 1944

12-1-44

Nothing today.

12-2-44

Went to Blecheimmer [sic Blechhammer] today. Saw flak that made Vienna and Munich look sick. It wasn't at all good. We were quite lucky to get thru the stuff looked solid enough to walk on, but was about 200 feet below us. Our Colonel got his no 4 engine shot out and lost his hydraulic system. We only got a few holes in our ship.

The B17's had been over the target ahead of us and the smoke went way up above us. It was so thick when we went thru you could hardly stay in formation.

12-3-44

Were briefed for our first real milk run today but didn't get off because of weather.

12-4-44

Had a standown today to receive the Presidential Citation for a raid the Sqdn pulled on Vienna before we got here. Had a big dress parade with all the trimmings. First one since cadets.

12-5-44

Were briefed for Lenz today, but again didn't get off because of weather. Laid around and read.

12-6-44

Were briefed for a milk run to Brataislava, Austria today and flak wasn't too bad but it was no milk run. We were jumped by fighters as we came off the target and they made passes at our formations for 45 min to an hour on the way back. Our P38's which were supposed to give us cover finally showed up and ran them away. We saw two B24's go down, most of their crews bailing out and four fighters, ME 109's, go down.

They didn't actually attack our ship, but we were sure they would any time. Our tail gunner fired at four of them as they were starting in, he says, and they changed their minds when they saw the tracers.

Back in Yougoslavia and over the Adriatic, we encountered a lot of weather. The formation finally dived thru a hole and came home under it about 1000 feet above the water.

Cy was stick today and I worked especially hard. Am very tired tonite.

<u>12-7-44</u>

We were not scheduled to do anything today. Should have started to Bari or Naples on our 3 day pass that starts tomorrow, but just didn't feel like it. Maggie & I will go to Bari tomorrow I think. Cy is going to stick around and try to get doctored up. He can't sleep at night.

12-8-44 to 12-10-44

Had a good time in Bari. Maggie and I couldn't get a room in the hotels so the Red Cross gave us a list of rooms in private residences. The one we went to was ok and the lady had three pretty nice daughters who wanted us to stay with them in the evenings instead of going to town. We played ping pong, rummy and danced. They had a good radio and record player and most of the popular American records. Don't know where they got the records.

The records had to be changed each time as all Italian equipment is years behind. I'd like to go see them again if I get a couple of days off. They asked us to be sure and come back for Xmas & new years.

The girls are very educated and speak good English as well as two or three other languages. Some of them have been in the states.

I forgot to write that on the take-off for the mission on 12-6-44 a ship blew up at the end of the runway. We took off thru the black smoke of the explosion. There was nothing of the ship left that you couldn't put in a bushel basket. When we returned and landed they still hadn't picked up the charred flesh and bits of bloody clothing.

12-11-44

Had a mission to Vienna today. It was a pretty good one. There was lots and lots of flak, but it happened to all be in the boxes above and below us. We came thru with only a few holes in the wings of the ship. Nothing at all serious.

I think we did a good job on the target. Dropped incendiaries, 1200 from our ship alone on the industrial area. Looked like the whole town was on fire when we left.

Got the radio from home today. Its wonderful to have it here.

12-12-44

Nothing today. Bad weather. Read magazines sent from home and listened to the radio. Just heard Red Skelton.

12-13-44

Were briefed for Brux Oil Refinery this morning but didn't have to go because of weather. That mission upset me pretty badly. Flak was worse than

Blechhammer, if possible, and we were to get the whole Luffwaf because the 8th AF couldn't operate because of weather. We were all plenty relieved when they called the mission off before the finished briefing.

12-14-44

We were scheduled again today, but the weather was so bad they did not even wake us.

Had a party at the club tonite with several English nurses imported. I enjoyed dancing with a Red Cross girl.

12-15-44

Got to bed at 0100 this morning and got up at 0300 to brief. Finally we got an easy mission. Didn't have any flak or fighters either. Bombed a railroad yard between Lenz [Linz] and Vienna, Austria.

Bombed thru an overcast so don't know how we did.

12-16-44

Nothing today.

12-17-44

Same.

12-18-44

Am writing this 1-2-45. Will try to recall dates and events as well as possible.

Took off for Belechhimmer North Oil Refinery today. It's over 700 miles each way and is supposed to be the worst target we have.

We got an old ship "White L." No 3 engine vibrated badly all the way getting worse all the time, but not bad enough to "early return."

Over the target we got some very close flak and tho, to our knowledge, none hit the fusalauge the engines were riddled.

We lost and feathered no 2 on the rally off the target but stayed with the formation for protection from fighters, down to the Yougoslavia border where no 4 engine ran out of oil and stopped. Since there was no oil the prop would not feather and "ran away." It was turning about 3000 RPM and looked like it would shake the wing off and we could do nothing.

We were still over enemy territory and had 20000 feet altitude so we stayed with the ship.

The situation got no worse for about an hour except that we lost altitude slowly, and we were pulling the remaining engines very hard.

Being above the overcast, we were not sure of our exact position but knew we were near the coast. We decided to try and make the air strip on the isle of Vis near the Yougo. coast.

About this time the two remaining engines began to peter out, and we could only get around 25" of mercury out of them. This made us lose altitude at 700 ft/min. With these engines getting worse and no 3 still running and vibrating so badly, we were afraid to go thru the overcast which was below the mountain tops and look for the island. The strip there is surrounded by mountains and is a man killer anyway.

I saw water thru a break below us and since we didn't want to jump in the water, we turned around and headed in the direction of land alt 15000 feet.

We went thru one layer of clouds and flew for, I guess 10 or 15 min till I saw thru a break mountains and snow. At this point we started jumping out. Alt 8,500 feet – highest mountains on map 6000 feet. The crew was all lined up on the cat walk and went out in rapid succession.

During the time after our second engine went out, I'd been talking to "Air Sea rescue" and they had gotten fixes etc on us. I told them we were bailing, left the seat got my .45 and in on and waited on Cy on the catwalk.

We had always said if we ever jumped we'd do it together if possible. He came out to the catwalk (we had the ship on auto pilot) and said he was ready.

I had surprising little fear at jumping. Simply put my head down and rolled forward from a standing position off the catwalk. When I saw the ship going away from me I pulled very hard on the rip cord. So hard, in fact, that it was thrown out of my hand in the motion and I saw it falling.

The ensuing jerk was surprisingly violent. In fact it seemed to me it rattled my teeth; but it was after all, the most pleasant jerk I've ever felt.

One of the straps was on a testical and I tried to get it off but could not, so resolved to ride it down since the pain, while present, was not too severe.

I looked for Cy but could not see him; the plane was turning crazily and going down. After a short time I saw him fall from the bomb bay and was relieved to see his chute open. He later said he watched my jump then looked at the ground and became scared thus the hesitation. I don't blame him much.

Shortly after this the stillness (its very, very quiet after the chute opens) was broken by the sound of the ship hitting the ground. Sounded like a tin roof being hit with a falling tree.

I called to Cy but heard no answer. He said he heard me and answered. Then I went into a cloud and got into a lot of turbulence. It started me to swinging violently and at times I thought I was going up. Before then I had been trying to keep track of the direction Cy was from me and the direction of the sun so I'd have an idea about the best direction to start walking but in the cloud I lost track of every thing. Also before the cloud I'd had time to try to slip the chute just to see if I could control it. The theory being to pull the risers on the side toward the direction you want to go thus spilling air out the other side of the chute and moving you in the desired direction. Being above the cloud I had no reference point and couldn't tell how I was doing.

When I broke out of the cloud I saw the top of a large pine tree very near and pointing right at my solar plexis. I grabbed the risers in front of me and gave a heave. The next thing I knew I was up to my thighs in a big snow drift beside the tree. The chute had caught in the lower limbs and some what broken the fall. The snow also helped, but I hit pretty hard. I know I increased my speed by pulling the risers when I did, but that may or may not have kept me out of the tree top.

I discovered I was not hurt, but the place sure looked desolate. I was on top of a mountain covered with pine trees and snow. The surrounding mountains shut off the sun and I did not know what direction was what.

The army says to keep your chute with you for warmth, bandages etc but mine was in the tree and I had no knife (a sad discovery) to cut it out with. My .45 was a great comfort. I looked at my watch and it was exactly 3:00 PM.

I removed my chute harness and "may west" and started to walk in the direction that looked easiest and less thickly covered with trees down the side of the mountain. I could have gone down any side as I was right on top. I put a cartridge in the chamber of my .45 as I did not know who or what I'd see.

I hadn't gone far before I saw thru a hole in the trees a sorta valley or clear place between the mountain and another one and a very sharp roofed building, like a very small barn.

I guess it took me an hour to get there and on the way I saw where someone had gotten wood and saw another building similar to the first.

The first proved to be a barn and a peasant woman was there milking goats. I didn't know just how to approach her, but I guess I did the only thing I could do. I walked up behind her and said "Americano" and extended my hand to shake when she turned around. She seemed friendly and said "Yougoslav" and got up and shook my hand. Her hand was covered with wet cow dung. I wiped mine off on my electric flying pants.

The woman pointed to the other building and indicated that I should go there, but I guess I looked so dumb she decided to go with me. On the way she she showed me a patch of snow that was covered with tracks and made motions that caused me to know Cy had landed there. When we got to the house (I call it that) Cy was there almost vomiting over some sour goats milk full of scum and strings and a hunk of stuff that served as bread.

We were quite glad to see each other and somewhat lucky too. At the house were three men, two more women, and three babies, two big enough to sit up and one in a cradle.

Cy said they were friendly and had given him food he could not eat but didn't want to offend them. The people were in rags and did not seem to mind the cold that was beginning to bother me since I had stopped walking. They had pointed in the direction of each town Cy had read from the map and thus pretty well located us on it. We guessed we were 100 miles inland and quite a ways from any decent road thru the Dinaric Alps that were between us and the sea. We foolishly thought it would take us at the most 2 days to walk to Split.

We did not know with what group the people were affiliated but they were friendly to us Americans, which they identified by Air Corps patches on our clothes.

They took us back into the house and put the sour milk and so called bread before us. I don't know how to describe the bread but should try because it was our main source of existence for 10 days.

I don't know what grain its made from but the stuff is very black, much blacker than any wheat I ever saw and is either very soggie, in the middle, or so hard you have to use your back teeth to bite it on the crust. It has no seasoning whatsoever but even so I don't see how any grain could taste so badly. It tastes sour so much so, in fact, that it makes your tongue smart.

Anyway, we ate a little of it and drank a good bit of the stringy milk with a wooden spoon out of a wooden bowl, both using the same bowl. Later the rest of the family ate from the same bowl with the same two spoons.

The house was made of logs and had shingles very similar to the ones used on barns back home on the roof. There was nothing in the loft, it being reserved for the smoke which was let out every now and then when it got too bad thru a sorta butterfly valve arrangement in the roof which was worked by means of a long pole.

There were two rooms in the house one contained the fire and the goats and cow. The cooking was done here. There was no floor and the only excess to the second room was thru this first one.

The second room was very small, with a ceiling, very low, a floor and was heated by an ingenious clay attachment on the back of the chimney which, as I said, only went up to the loft.

We sat around on the floor for a while then [I] indicated that we were sleepy. One of the men took me out to show him my tracks in the snow so he could go for my chute. When I came back, they had spread some straw out on the floor and Cy was laying down on it. We laid there a couple of hours, but could not sleep.

The guy came back with my chute and we sat us and talked for a couple of hours. The people were very curious about our clothes chutes etc. The shoes were the things of biggest interest. They wanted to feel all our clothes right down to the underwear and work all zippers, hooks, fasteners etc.

The conversation was very limited. They would take a piece of candy I happened to have in my jacket pocket and say "Yougoslav 'bon-bon.' Americano...?" We'd say "Americano 'candy.'" Then we'd point to a shoe and say "Americano 'shoe.' Yougoslov...?" They'd give the Yougo name etc. After [a] while we did get sleepy enough to lay down. The rest of them, all nine, slept on the floor of the same room. It was quite full.

I could feel bugs and things crawling all over me and was able to kill by squashing several of them on my forehead and other exposed portions of my body.

When the mother of the baby wanted to feed it, instead of taking it up she just got down on her knees beside the cradle and leaned over it.

Everyone had colds and spat and blew their noses on the floor, walls or whatever was easiest. They all slobbered profusely and would only bother to wipe their chins when the excretion became uncomfortably cold or got in the way.

12-19-44

Next morning we woke very early covered in bed bug bites etc and got a candle lit. The others finally got up and brought out some more of the same food. We ate very little. The man of the house said he'd take us to Split (on the coast) and we got ready to go. Cy gave them all of his chute, his flying boots, which were too heavy to walk in, and some other stuff he couldn't carry. I gave him half of my chute and my heavy electric flying pants as they were much too heavy to walk in. I had to keep the jacket as I had nothing else.

He walked with us about two miles to another house where we set about two hours till three or four Partisen's with Red stars on their caps come and started off with us. The family at this house was much the same as the first and wanted to play with our clothes just as the others did.

On the way to the house we saw where the ship had crashed but didn't go over. I felt that the sight would be quite depressing and I wanted to get started to Split.

At the house we saw the peasants carrying self sealing gas tanks, flak suits oxygen bottles, and all sorts of stuff.

They even brought a 100 lb self computing gun sight out of the Martain Turret in for us to tell them what it was. The housing was broken and they could see all the cog wheels etc and so wouldn't believe us when we indicated it was a sight.

All the people we saw were friendly. Americano seems to be the magic word there.

Finally, we started walking with three or four Partisins. We walked an hour or so and another Partisen caught us and took us right back the way we'd come, past the airplane etc.

We walked the rest of the day behind him over mountains, and very rough country. At 1:00 o'clock we came to a sorta village and were told that the rest of the crew had been there the night before and had started on that morning. Also that two of them had broken legs and were on horses. Those people all had red stars and guns and hand granades. All the time I was in Yougo I saw no Partisen without granades on his belt.

The people brought out some bread and put a bowl of clabber milk between us. We ate a good bit of it as we were quite hungry.

This was the first place we saw girl soldiers. Here and everywhere else about 15% of the Partisen's were women and they did just as the men did and were dressed and armed the same.

We left there and walked till 5:30 PM.. I've never been so tired. When we got the next town where we were to catch the rest of the crew and the house where they were was only 50 feet away I still didn't know whether I could make it or not. I did tho and was glad to find the boys and they were glad to see us. Jay and Harry had broken legs and Jay swore he would never ride another mule.

All the country we came thru this day bore the works of war. All buildings had been burned. Only churches remained. The town we were in, Kuprus, had been completely destroyed. No roof in the downtown area remained and the town was deserted except for a very few people on the edges and the small band of Partisins.

These people were very good to us but wanted our watches and .45's. They got my gun but I managed to keep my watch. I wanted it as it was my civilian watch my G. I. one being back at the tent.

They gave us the best food they had, but I couldn't eat at night as I was too tired. I drank some water and fell asleep on the floor where we slept.

12-20-44

They again gave us the best food they had which was a platter of very very greasy meat chips. I don't know what kind. And some hot goats milk. I ate a lot this morning. It was the only really big amount of food I ate the whole trip. I got started on the old greasy meat and couldn't stop.

I forgot to mention that I had opened my parachute first aid kit and taken the morphene out before I gave it away. Some of it had leaked out but they gave the rest of it to Jay during the night. He had one shot during the day. That finished our morphene and as far as I know Harry didn't get any.

Cy and I tried to argue the Comisiar into sending the boys on in a wagon or on a sled but he indicated that it was impossible because of the road blocks. We later found he was exactly right.

About 10:30 we started up the mountain with three or four partisans and leading the donkeys with Jay

& Harry. It was a very nerve wracking day. We crossed two high mountains following the road part way and paths part way.

The roads had been blown up and had trees cut across them so that the entire distance was one detour after another. The snow was drifted and when the little mules went thru a drift the broken legs drug and if the animals stumbled as they frequently did, they kicked the legs.

At one place it looked completely hopeless. Harry's horse was kicking his foot at every step. Hahn and I who were with Harry finally had to take him off and I put long splints over the others thus immobilizing his leg to the hip. I didn't think it would help much but it did the trick and we were able to catch the other boys.

One time Jay's horse fell with him in a snow drift. Jay screamed very loudly. The boys had to carry him on thru. We carried Harry all the way thru because it was an especially bad drift. The effort completely winded me and I had to rest and catch the others later.

We passed some abanden German trucks along the read.

We finally came out of the mountains and came to a very nice town, comparatively speaking, about 5 or 5:30 PM.

Here we slept in a Partisan dispensary and were again treated well. As alway they gave us the best food they had but it was the same as before except we had soup once.

In the evening they brought in a man who spoke very good English. I can't say how wonderful it was to hear him. He told us we were to be put on a train and sent north to another town where there was a hospital.

The man's name was Joe Jerek. Joe and his wife had been in Detroit for 17 years. He said his wife called him and said she heard someone speak English. Seems as we passed his house in the evening someone had called out "How would you like to have a shot now?" and she heard it.

Joe took four of us up to his house tonite to meet his wife. We stayed an hour and Maggie and a couple of boys had drinks and I drank some delicious butter milk. Their home was very modern for there and much like some I've seen in the states.

We slept on some straw on the floor of the dispensary. The sick boys had beds.

12-21-44

Joe came back this morning and asked some of us to come home with him for breakfast. I went and had a wonderful one. Had eggs sunny side up.

We went to catch the train at 10:00 AM but the train didn't come till 7:00 PM so we spend the day with Joe seeing the town. Its name was Bologanice and it was a very nice town in peace time. It had been shot up pretty badly tho and where flowers and shrubs had been was just mud.

We saw where 500 lb bombs had hit, very fortunately, in a football field. (Joe said they have football here.) Saw bunkers (air raid shelters) the Germans had built. Also met Joe's daughter and grandson. The daughter spoke good English and was very well read. Her husband had been executed by the Germans.

Joe changed some money for us and we bought apples and nuts that really tasted good. We had $48.^{00} in American money in our escape kits.

At 7:00 PM we carried the boys to the station and got in a box car. The train goes no faster than you can walk on very narrow gage tracks. Anyway they had a stove and straw in the car and it wasn't too bad. We reached Jajce about 11:30 or 12:00 PM and were met at the train by Partisans with streachers. They carried the boys and we walked about a mile thru narrow streets to the hospital.

Here a fat Partisan doctor with a handle bar mustache set the boys legs and splinted them. Most of his help was pretty sharp looking girls. When he finished with them, two of the girls carried them and put them in a ward full of men and boys with cosely cut hair.

About 3:00 AM he finished and we had tea, which was very good, and brown bread, which was very bad, with him. Then we left the hospital and went to see the Comisar. He gave a soldier an order and we followed him. We went to an old man and woman's house and the soldier beat on the door with his rifle butt till he got them out and got in. Among many protests we slept in the kitchen on the floor after running the old woman out. Of course we didn't want to do this but could only do as the soldier said. He indicated that they were German sympathisers.

12-22-44

When we woke up the old folks were much more friendly and tried to get us to give them some parachute silk. We didn't.

We went back to the hospital on the hill and were fed hot soup and sat around there in a ward all day. The work there was done by girls many of whom had been wounded in battle and were recovering there.

We got acquainted with a pilot who had flown Darnier airplanes. Later met another one in this same town who spoke a little English. He had flown pursuit ships for Germany till he and a few others were ordered to attack a formation of 400 heavy bombers. He deserted and came to Yougo.

In the evening we again were taken to the Comisiar and sat in his outer office for a couple of hours. Then we were taken to the officer's mess for supper. The rest of the stay there we ate in this mess and the food was always the same. Soup and black bread. We learned to eat a few bits of bread in the soup.

After supper we were very happy to be given a large room with beds and a stove.

We slept with our clothes on two in a twin bed made of boards and corn shucks.

12-23-44

Were told we'd get a car to Sanshi Mas where there was an air strip but we never did. In fact the only car we saw in this town was a big black one belonging to one of the high officials which they pushed to get started every morning. This town reminded me very very much of Winona, W. Va. Except for a wall around part of the town and the buildings being of the customary European masonry and a bit taller in the center of the town, there was little difference in the appearance.

We were greatly impressed with the people. They were suffering untold hardships and were taking it on the chin and laughing.

We ate three meals and laid around the room all day. Some of the boys went to town and got more apples and nuts. Made a couple of trips to the hospital to see the boys.

We were told we might possibly leave tomorrow.

12-24-44

Spent the day much like yesterday. Behind the hospital on the hillside there stood, when we came, a large swatsika behind which was a little graveyard of, I guess, a hundred crosses. The Germans had been in this town very recently.

Today when I went to see the boys, two buxom Partisan girls were in the grave yard laughing and talking and singing as they chopped down the crosses for fire wood. I imagine the swatsika will go too as it was made of wood also.

About 5:00 PM we were told to get ready to go and we were very happy. We stopped at the Comisiars again and he gave me a paper with my name and I don't know what else on it. I guessed rightly that it was some kind of transportation order.

We were then started toward the railroad station with a soldier. We didn't see anything of Jay and Harry and protested but got no where. I started to the hospital, but was stopped by the soldier. When I insisted, he indicated that Jay & Harry were already on the train.

On the way to the train he stopped at several bakeries and finally found one that had some of the old black bread and requisitioned at least 50 lbs of it. He put it in a burlap sack. I ran ahead and bought 10 kilos of apples and took off my electric flying jacket to put them in when I saw him getting all that bread.

We got to the station and found the little old train and station so crowded we couldn't have gotten near it except for the little soldier and the magic word "Americano."

The train was already loaded, but they unloaded nine people from a box car and put us and our soldier on. We saw nothing of Harry and Jay and knew it was impossible for them to travel on this train. I had time to write them a note dark tho it was, and Rabbit who had learned a bit more of the language than the rest of us, got it to a girl with instructions to deliver it right away.

The box car was so tightly packed you could hardly find room for your feet and no one could sit down. We did manage to take turns sitting on the sack of bread after the train started and things got settled a bit.

The train was primarily a troop train and the soldiers sang continually which became extremely aggravating to us. We couldn't understand the words and the music, if any, was all the same and very corny. About 10% of their soldiers are women. The women are treated the same as the men and carry grenades on their belts, dress the same, sleep on the ground with the men and all. I never saw anything relating to, or indicating sexual relations among them. The men answered calls of nature away from the train in the bushes instead of right in the tracks as they ordinarily would have. They asked, thru an old soldier who could speak a little English, us to sing some songs for them. The boys sang a few songs for them. "Pistol Packing Mama, Air Corps Song, I've Been Working on the R. R. etc."

The train moved for about 10 min then broke down for an hour, then it moved for three or four hours and broke down again. The soldiers all got off and cut wood for the engine and pushed the train up a hill. About 1:00 AM the engine put us on a siding and went for water. We were about to freeze so when the English speaking man said to come with him and he'd find a house we were indeed happy to go.

We followed him up the hill to a house where he aroused an old woman who let us in and made a fire. The man produced from his pack a bottle from which he and some of the boys partook and some white goats cheese, which smelled and tasted much like limburger, but which we all ate and enjoyed.

I think we all passed out right there because the next thing I knew the man was shaking me saying we should go as the engine was back. I woke everyone and looked at my watch. It was 3. A. M.

12-25-44

When we got to the train we found it was not ready to go but had to go down to the bottom of the mountain and bring up part of the cars it had left there. We went into another house which was as full of people as the box car had been and stayed an hour or so. The house was warm and the people were friendly and the girls wanted to feel us and our clothes which wasn't too unpleasant, crowded tho it was. The train was finally ready and we got started again about daylight. All morning we moved for about 5 minutes and stopped to cut wood and get up steam for 15 min. We were all very cold and dejected. The bugs and lice were still on us and we were filthy, tired, sleepy, cold, homesick on Christmas Day and needed shaves. My mustache was hanging down in my mouth.

About noon they put us on a siding and said we would be there a while. The while turned out to be about 3 hours. Maggie built a fire which turned out to b a good idea.

By now all our apples were gone and we were pretty hungry. The head man of the Partisan soldiers came to our rescue with a small can of corn beef which had been dropped to them by allies. That corn beef, tho there was hardly enough to go around, tasted wonderful. It was our Christmas dinner.

Finally another train came along and hooked onto our car and a couple of others. It was a little better and went a little farther between stops for wood and to get up steam. As we got higher into the mountains they could shovel snow into the engine instead of going for water so often.

At the last stop we had to change from the box car to a flat car. It was very cold and windy on the flat. I made friends with the engineer at one stop and got to ride some of the way in the engine. The engine was warm, but the steam got me damp and I was colder when I got off.

At dark the engine just poo'd out and couldn't go any farther. They said it was 7 kilometers farther to the top of the mountain and the soldiers were going to walk. We walked too and took turns carrying the sack of bread. We wanted to leave it but the little soldier wouldn't hear of it.

At the top of the mountain we saw truck tracks in the snow. I think that was the most welcome sight we'd seen. A little farther on we saw the trucks. It was a very moon light night.

The trucks were pretty well loaded when we got there and there were still lots of soldiers to get on. We thought we were in trouble again for a while when the paper the man had given me didn't produce immediate results. Finally tho when the soldiers all got on they let us scatter out and get on the trucks a couple at a time. Cy, Monty, and I got on the same one. The trucks wee Dodges the British had let the Partisians have. The Partisians are the poorest of poor drivers.

The truck was, if possible, more crowded then the box car was. I don't know how we made the trip cause the next thing I knew we were in another

Comisar's office in Lavena. They gave us some greasy meat and bread. After that the three of us fell asleep in his office. When we awoke the other trucks, which had had trouble, had come and the other boys were there. It was 1:30 AM.

12-26-44

We got back on the trucks and went to another town where they let us sleep on the floor in a room where a lot of Partisian drivers and motor pool personnel were doing the same. One of them spoke a little English. We got to sleep again about 3:30 and were awakened about 7:00. They fed us some soup and finally got us in another truck (the soldiers went somewhere else earlier) with another Pilot and Co-pilot who had bailed out and had been traveling just ahead of us this far, and took us to a pretty good town (for Yougo) called Singe. We got there about 11:00 AM. We crossed very rough country which was completely covered with protruding rocks. I'd hate to bail out here, tho it is in open populated country, because of the rocks. The road had such sharp turns getting up and down the mountains that the guy had to back up two and three times to get around them.

At Singe we went to another Comisiar's office and were well treated. He called in a barber and we all got a shave. Then we had a good meal and were sent to a hotel.

They also brought in an interpreter. He was a beggar, but we didn't mind giving him things as we needed his services badly. He exchanged some money for us at much better rate than we had gotten before.

We were again treated well at the hotel, which had been badly bombed and had only a few serviceable rooms remaining and a bar in front and the family's rooms in the back.

We met an old man who also spoke English here and became more attached to him than our other interpreter. We were taken into the families dining room in the back and sat around talking to them thru our elderly friend. When we asked to be put to bed we were told the beds weren't ready. When they were ready the people said we had just as well wait to eat. We did so and sat down to a good meal of beef, potatoes, beans, and wine. The family was very nice and didn't have to put out the best they had as they did. They seemed to have four daughters who were very busy in the bar and fixing beds for us all that afternoon and evening but who we saw and talked to in the morning. The family asked many questions and, as everyone we met in Yougo, wanted to know had we ever bombed Yougo.

We were shown to rooms and a good bed each shortly after supper. I slept well, but some of the boys were sick to the stomach as was the case every night in Yougo.

12-27-44

When I woke up the others in my room were gone and a girl was shaking me. She motioned for me to get up. I said "dobria" (o.k.) and started to wait till she left. She did not leave, but kept insisting that I get up. I did, and dressed while she waited and escorted me downstairs. The others were there and we had breakfast. Also our military escort and the old gentleman we had met the night before were there. He was going to Split and wanted to go with us.

We got to the train station which was again crowded, but the paper did the trick again and we soon had a box car to ourselves except for a woman on a stretcher and her doctor.

Oh yes, before we left the hotel the girl who woke me asked, thru the old man, if I was married. I was quite surprised and flattered.

We were on the train about 1 ½ hours before it moved. We crossed the same barren, rock covered type mountains and got to Split about 2:30 PM.

Split is a very, very good town for Yougo. Is much like Bari. Has a beautiful harbor and bay.

We got off the train and were wandering more or less aimlessly up the water front street, our soldier boy being a green country boy, when we met a Jeep with an American shave tail. He wanted to know what the hell we represented. Guess we were a funny looking bunch. Our feet and legs were so sore, we were all limping.

He wanted to take us immediately to a boat that was leaving for the isle of Viss, but the Partisian Soldier had to find his superior and turn us over to him. This accomplished we were taken to British Air Sea Rescue boat, given a K ration and bar of peanut candy, and taken to Viss. The K-ration was very very good and after it I enjoyed the boat ride, it being my first.

At Viss we were taken to a mess line and had a good meal from mess kits. Had our first coffee that was coffee for 10 days. Later we slept on a cot in the attic of one of the building on the water front. It was cold, but we had plenty of blankets.

<u>12-28-44</u>

Got up at 7:00 and had breakfast from mess kits again. I wandered along the water front for a while. In peace time this must have been a beautiful island. The water is the clearest I've ever seen. Where a large steamer was sitting it looked only 2 feet deep. but couldn't have been less than 10. I was told later by a Sgt. that it was 25 feet where it looked like 4 or 5.

About 8 o'clock we were taken to an air strip and sat around there till 11:30 when a C 47 came in and got us. We were lucky to get on board as some had to wait on the next ship.

At Bari we were taken to an army hospital where we were fed and got a bath and pajamas and parted with our old clothes which were to be de-loused. After our baths, we de-loused ourselves with a spray gun and powder. We slept in a large tent.

12-29-44

Slept most of the morning except for long enough to get an army issue of clothes and pick up our deloused ones. In the afternoon we went down to 15th AF Hq's. and were interrogated.

Stayed in town tonite and I went over and visited my Italian friends. We had a room at the army hotel.

12-30-44

A truck came for us about 1:00 PM and we came home. Have had a hell of a time getting the new crew moved out of our tent and our stuff moved back in. Its wonderful to be home. This mess line is what I've been dreaming of.

12-31-44

Slept all day except for time enough to eat and get payed. I cabled Mother tho I wasn't supposed to.

Also wrote her Special Del. 12- 29-44. We were told they sent out m.i.a. reports when we'd been down 48 hours.

Charles A. Haynes—Fresh Out of Training

The B-24, "Flying Boxcar" Crew.
Pilot, Curtis I. Eatman (front row, 2nd from r.)
Co-pilot, Charles A. Haynes (front row, r.)

Chuck Haynes, standing, 2nd from the right; Curtis Eatman, squatting, 1st on the left.

The jaunty aviator, Charles "Chuck" Haynes!

"ME" – Chuck, shortly after WW II

Charles and Kathryn, July 1978

Betty Eatman/Haynes

Kathryn and Charles, Reunited

Curtis & Betty Eatman – February 1978

Elizabeth L. "Betty" Eatman
and
Charles A. "Chuck" Haynes

are pleased to
announce their marriage
on
September 12, 1998

They will be at home at
Rt. 3, Box 158
Eutaw, Alabama 35462
(205) 372-4449

The Happy Couple, September 12, 1998

Charles & Betty [Eatman] Haynes – September 1983

Charles and son David – June 2005

Charles & Betty – June 2005

January 1945

[From September to December 1944, I took the entries verbatim from Charles Haynes original handwritten notes. From this point on, however, only a typewritten transcription is available, produced sometime later. It differs in some respects to the original notes, quite possibly due to Charles Haynes's own desire to "clean it up a bit," or due to transcription errors by the typist. Therefore, having the original entries alongside part of the typed manuscript, allowed the following entries to reflect the style used previously, with only *slight* changes and adaptations to synchronize the following notes with previous ones and to preserve the author's "voice" throughout. – T. H. Pine]

1-1-45

Slept and wrote letters today. Getting over our missing in action experience in Yougoslavia.

1-2-45

Same as yesterday.

[You'll recall, Charles wrote the long entry for December 18th—the day his bomber went down—on this day. – T. H. Pine]

1-3-45

I went into Bari today. Got a room at the home of the Italian family with whom I've been staying. Played records and danced in the evening.

1-4-45

Still in Bari. Wrote several letters in the Red Cross Club. Listening to the radio, played records and danced again.

1-5-45

Came home today. I was lucky and caught a ride in a truck cab right up to the gate. Had a letter from Lyle while I was gone.

1-6-45

We got issued flying equipment again today. We lost practically everything we had when we went down. Guess we're all set to fly again. They have assigned two new men to our crew to replace the ones we had to leave at Yougo.

1-7-45

Went to church this morning.

1-8-45

Nothing today except got a reissue of flying equipment still needed.

1-9-45

I got sick this afternoon. Am taking the flu I think. Stepped outside the tent tonite and fainted. An enlisted man carried me inside and put me on the bed.

1-10-45

Spent a very bad nite last nite. Had temperature and my back hurt badly. Feel much better tonite though. The boys have been carrying my meals to me.

Got a letter from Mr. and Mrs. Eatman asking me to write them about Cy. They got m.i.a. report on January 2.

1-11-45

I think I'm about over the flu. Stayed in today and read and slept.

We had about three inches of snow last nite. It's very sloppy. Cy went to town to see Harry and Jay, who are in the hospital in Bari.

1-12-45

I'm still D. N. I. F. but feeling much better. Stayed in bed. I'm pretty blue about lack of mail.

1-13-45

Same as yesterday. The boys got up to fly. Had another co-pilot. They did not take off, however. I got assigned back to duty tonite.

1-14-45

Got up and were briefed but didn't get off. We had a meeting in the club and caught hell from the CO about lack of military courtesy and discipline in us and the crews.

1-15-45

Same as yesterday. The weather is still bad. Saw a film this morning on the B 29. It's quite different. Don't think I like it.

1-16-45

Maggie and I went to Bari to see Jay and Harry. They are in good spirits. Are going to the states in two weeks.

We spend the evening at the Terzulli's again and had a very pleasant time. Had to stand in the rain from 8:30 till 11:30 PM waiting for a truck to come home in. I drove it part way home. The driver got sleepy.

1-17-45

Nothing today. Our orders to Cairo and Palestine for rest leave came thru yesterday. Bad weather today. If it's better tomorrow we'll go.

We've received no mail for almost two weeks. My last letter from home was dated December 21. After each mail call, or time for mail call each evening, we're very depressed.

1-18-45

Weather was no good this morning so we slept again. It's much better tonite. I'm guessing we'll get off for Cairo tomorrow.

I got three very welcome letters today.

1-19-45

Got off around 7:00 AM. Had some bad weather en route but a fairly pleasant ride. Another ship from our group who was going with us got lost in the weather and landed 400 miles short of Cairo at a British field.

We got here about 2:00 PM and got rooms at a small hotel. There are many autos here, mostly American. You can get a taxi any time. Prices are exorbitant.

1-20-45

The guides and draggerman have been annoying us to death. We just looked around town and took things easy today.

Went to the PX and got some stuff and bought the boots the boys at the base asked us to get for them.

Cairo has much of the old and much of the new. It's a very quaint place. We saw the tombs of the last four kings of Egypt in a very large and beautiful mosque.

1-21-45

Today we engaged a guide and went out to see the pyramids and the sphinx. I guess they are quite wonderful but I wasn't so greatly impressed. Rode camels around the pyramids and between them and the sphinx. We also took pictures and picked up stones etc.

We've been eating steak about three times a day here. It's very good at the St. James Restaurant.

1-22-45

Everyone decided to go to Palestine today, so we took off around 11:30 AM and got here about 1:00. On the take-off a musketo [Mosquito bomber] taxied across in front of us and we missed him by inches.

Tel Aviv is a very nice town. More like the states than anything I've seen. Wide streets, beautiful buildings, and lots of autos. We have a very nice room at the Yarden Hotel. The women here are beautiful.

1-23-45

All the boys got drunk last night, so this morning we all slept in for a change.

This afternoon we just loafed around and looked the town over. All prices here are unreasonable. Breakfast cost me $3.00.

Baby carriages seem to be the big business here. I've never seen so many on the street. The stores and shops are very modern and have beautiful things, for a price.

1-24-45

Slept in again this morning, then just played around town all day. It's very pleasant here.

1-25-45

Same as yesterday. Signed up for a Red Cross Tour tomorrow.

1-26-45

Went to Jerusalem today. We saw the Mount of Olives, the Gardens of Gethsemane, The Holy

Sepulchre, the path of Christ from the court of Pilot to the cross etc. It was a very good trip.

This part of the country is the most fertile and nicest of any I've seen. Saw many orange orchards with the largest fruit I've ever seen.

1-27-45

Today we flew back to Cairo. Are staying at the same hotel.

This afternoon I got back to the PX and bought some bracelets, etc. to give to my sisters. We're sort of tired and are turning in early tonite. Must start to Italy tomorrow, weather permitting.

1-28-45

We did return to Italy today, tho we didn't make it quite home. The weather was the best possible the first half of the trip but as we neared Italy it got very bad. We flew on the deck to keep out of clouds. Got up to Barletta before it got absolutely zero zero then turned back and landed at Bari. We're staying here tonight.

I got beds for the officers at my friends the Terzullis. It's rainy and bad. Cy, Maggie and Rabbit went to the hospital to see Jay and Harry.

1-29-45

Today we got cleared to go home but the weather was very very bad. We took off, like damn fools, in a snow storm, and were out of sight of the ground almost before I got the wheels up.

Cy buzzed ground trying to find the ground for a while and sacred us all badly before we climbed thru the weather. We luckily found a hole to come down thru. The place is desolate, cold and muddy but it's good to be back and have lots of mail.

1-30-45

Had a lecture on weather today and I cleaned up my part of the tent. My personal belongings were in bad shape.

The weather has been so bad the outfit has flown only one sortie while we were gone. They went to Lenz and got badly shot up. Only one boy I knew was killed tho. I surely hope the Russians keep going. They seem to be our salvation. I mailed Sue a watch and Mother a pair of hose today.

1-31-45

We had 6 hours of school today. There's a mobil training unit here teaching a lot of good stuff on new additions to, and modifications of the B 24. We're scheduled to fly tomorrow.

From the Farm to the Cockpit

I mailed the souvenirs I got in Cairo today. Bracelets home to Jeanne and Louise, hose to Mother, and field jacket to Bill. Got paid tonite.

February 1945

2-1-45

We got a sortie today but didn't help the war effort any. Just flew around over Germany above an overcast trying to find Groz. All the Mickies went out and we finally bombed an open field and came home.

No mail for three days now.

2-2-45

Just laid around today. Sent Peggy $130.00 and Mother $100.00. Got a letter from Mother, Peggy and John.

2-3-45

We had an inspection of all our quartermaster issue this morning. Have lots of rumors that we will move soon. I hope so. No theater could be worse than this.

This afternoon we had four hours of classes on modification of the B two dozen.

2-4-45

Went to church today.

2-5-45

Had a lecture on the C 1 auto pilot. Same stuff we had in the states.

Mailed Peggy a scarf from my parachute. Rabbit flew with another crew today. We are scheduled for tomorrow.

2-6-45

Did not get off. Just took it easy.

2-7-45

Bombed Vienna today. It was a rough deal. Had lots of weather on the way out. Flak was very bad. We picked up several holes in the ship, but fortunately none struck vital spots.

No mail tonite. 14th sortie.

2-8-45

Nothing today. Saw a show this afternoon. "Cassanova Brown" with Gary Cooper. It was good.

Got a letter from Dad and one from Jeanne.

2-9-45

Nothing today.

2-10-45

Had formation and was presented the Air Medal. Sent it to Mother.

2-11-45

Went to church.

2-12-45

Nothing today.

2-13-45

Rabbit flew with another crew. Went down flak alley in Vienna. Sure glad we didn't have to go. Guess we'll be up tomorrow.

We had a beautiful day today. Played baseball in our underwear and shoes only.

2-14-45

I flew thru the Vienna flak again today. Flew with Scott and Maggie flew with someone else. The other boys stayed at home. This makes 15 sorties.

Got a letter from home mailed Feb 4.

2-15-45

We bombed a rail yard 40 miles south of Vienna today. Had a real milk run. Saw no flak or fighters and had a brand new ship. It's really a honey. Flies almost as easy as an auto drives. Only drawback was the jerk leading the box flew thru clouds a couple of times. The box split up every way. We were quite lucky no two ships went the same way at the same time.

2-16-45

Nothing today.

2-17-45

Read Steinbecks "To A God Unknown" today. Got quite a kick out of it.

2-18-45

Started to Vienna with Scott again today but the whole wing had to turn back in the middle of Yougo because of clouds. We were in the clouds quite a while and it was very nerve wracking. I'm pretty disgusted because we didn't get any credit for it. Not even combat time. Just four hours of practice formation. We're scheduled tomorrow. Church tonite.

2-19-45

Bombed a marshling yard in Vienna with Scott today. Two whole groups dropped their bombs early and turned off. The flak was awful. Our box stayed on course and got a beautiful hit on the target. We brought back a picture. Had a very strong head wind and were in the flak eighteen minutes. Had a bad scare about our gas. Had just enough to get back. Lost one engine on the bomb run but got it back again and got home on it.

2-20-45

Had a lecture on the Pacific war, past and present today. Slept and read the rest of the time.

No Mail tonite.

2-21-45

Nothing today.

2-22-45

Had pictures made for our new A. G. O. cards. Tomorrow we're to work.

2-23-45

Went to bomb a small marshling yard (Wells) just west of Lenz, but couldn't get at it because of clouds and orders to bomb it visually only. Bombed Villach yards instead. The boys said we did a good job. We flew deputy box lead at the target. Came near to landing on another ship. Saw it barely in time to go around. Too close.

2-24-45

Had a big formation and a couple of guys from our Sqdn. Got a D. F. C. Got a batch of old mail tonite.

2-25-45

Went to church this morning and wrote letters and had a session here in the tent this afternoon. Got more old mail tonite. We're to fly tomorrow.

2-26-45

We got up early to fly and were briefed for a milk run, then just at start engines time they called a standown. So we came home and laid around all day. Guess we'll maybe go tomorrow.

2-27-45

We did go today and got a rough one. The flak was about the worst I've ever seen since Blechheimmer [Blechhammer]. Bombed Augsburg west of Munich. The ship was full of holes. Had the waist windows broken and several holes around them. Luckily, no vital part was hit. The damn stuff sounded like 50 cal ammunition going off all around you. Got one V mail tonite.

2-28-45

Nothing today. Played poker this afternoon and tonite. Won $25 this afternoon and lost $7 tonite.

March 1945

3-1-45

Went to Bari with the mess officer in a Jeep. Spent a very pleasant day.

Saw Jay at the hospital and stopped at the Terzulli's for a while. Also got some pictures developed.

3-2-45

Nothing today.

3-3-45

We're scheduled to fly today, but got a standown due to weather. Guess we'll go tomorrow.

3-4-45

We were briefed for a milk run, but got a bad ship so it wasn't so milky for us. Maggie didn't fly with us cause he isn't checked out on radar bombing and we were deputy lead. We lost a super charger on the way up and lost No 1 engine at the insertion point and left the formation. Salvoed the bombs and started home. 15 min later lost no 3 engine and took a heading for Pecs, Hungary about 20 miles behind the Russian lines.

We luckily weren't intercepted by fighters and found the fighter strip ok. Cy and I were both pretty shakey and made a rough landing but got down ok with no one hurt. Were taken to the Russian commander and questioned thru two interpreters. Then we were made to bathe and given Russian underwear for ours, then fed a fairly good meal and put to bed on a straw mattress in a school building.

<u>3-5-45</u>

The Russians treat us fine here. Feed us chicken, lots of wine and the best there is while they eat soup.

We wandered around town a while this morning but didn't see anything very interesting.

This afternoon we were taken to an auditorium with the other hospital patients and saw a Russian news real. They say we may leave tomorrow. I don't know where.

An American born doctor stopped in to see us this eve. Seems he came here to finish his education and got stuck.

3-6-45

Cy and Milakovic (bombardier replacing Maggie) went to the ship and got our parachutes and some clothes we wanted to take with us. We loaded in an open Model A ford truck about 10:00 AM and left, headed west.

Reached the Danube about 3:00 PM. It isn't very blue but it's quite muddy. About the size of the Knawha. We were held up quite a while for other trucks and a lot of cattle and sheep but finally got across a pontoon bridge into Baja to another town and found about 60 other airmen there, mostly American.

3-7-45

One boy here is from our Sqdn. He's a radar man that flew with us once. Went down two days before we did. We are to sleep in a former school building on straw on the floor. Some of the boys are sleeping out with families in town. We couldn't make any arrangements today, so we'll sleep in the straw again tonite.

The food is very bad. Black bread, barley soup (no barley) and sometimes tea. We bought eggs, 100 for $3.00 and are cooking them on a little stove we have here. It's very crowded. About 30 men in one room.

3-8-45

Milackovic, who speaks this language and German and I got out into town and found places for our crew to sleep. There are ten of us staying in four different homes. Milackovic and I are staying in a very nice home with a woman, her daughter, and son in law. Her husband and son are in the German army.

These people are very glad to have us. It protects them from the Russian who mistreats them. They give us their very best hoarded food which is a real treat after what we've had. This is a little town of farmers who formerly worked the rich surrounding land.

3-9-45

(From a poor memory on March 23) We were all told we might leave today, but no such luck. The lady gave us some wine and several loaves of hard crusted, but otherwise pretty good, bread and some salami to take with us. She and her daughter cried a little when we left and seemed quite happy when we returned. We talked for a couple of hours after supper. Again slept between feather mattresses.

3-10-45

After much ado and many delays the Russians got another Model A Ford truck to running and hauled us, about 20 at a time (there are 60 here from Italy) to a little narrow gauge railroad in Baja about ten miles west of here.

Baja has been badly bombed. In the R. R. yards where we got into the box cars we saw German prisoners handling much American made equipment. Saw whole cars of G. I. shoes just piled up loose.

Moved slowly out of Baja about 6:00 PM and spent the night in the box car.

3-11-45

Last night was bad. There was only room for a few to lay down at a time and when you did lay down you froze. There was a stove in the car, but it put out little heat and smoked badly. We popped our chutes and wrapped up in them.

Today we're in beautiful country, but see many wrecked buildings, trenched fields and burned and wrecked equipment and other marks of war.

3-12-45

Still on the train. Spent another hectic nite. The train moves about 10 MPH and is stopped about half of the time. Before we left Baja the Russians gave us a glass water bottle that holds about a pint. Whenever the train stops, we all run to fill the bottles. They've given us salami and brown bread which we are eating with gusto. Taste damn good when you're hungry. This eve we pulled into Timoshora, Rumania. The R. R. yards are badly bombed.

<u>3-13-45</u>

The Russians took us off the train last night and after much fumbling around which is characteristic. They put us in private residences – 1, 2, or 3 at a place.

Milakovic and I got in with a caretaker of a very large office building. His three rooms were in the basement. His wife was dead and the Russians had taken his 18 year old daughter away to work so he had adopted a wife and daughter.

This is a wonderful place to be. The people don't know whether we are British or Americans but they worship both.

3-14-45

The old man brought a radio out of hiding and his adopted daughter brought in a girlfriend and we all had a very pleasant time last night. We strolled around town and talked to people during the day. It's lots of fun.

You can't stop on the street because a crowd of people will gather and block traffic in just a couple of minutes. It's very funny to have a crowd of people following you as you walk the street, or to see your tail gunner with one. About one out of every five speak a little English and translate everything you say.

3-15-45

We are told we'll leave today for Bucharest. Everyone wants to stay here. I only want to go so I can let the folks at home know that I'm ok. We're supposed to be at the train station at 12:00 PM.

They held the train until 5:00 PM so they could get all the boys rounded up and aboard. Many were drunk and didn't give a damn and many just didn't give a damn. While here I payed $32.00 for a camera and 24 rolls of film. Also took many letters from people to mail to friends and families in the states.

3-16-45

This is a big town and certainly bears the marks of war. Has been much bombed. The train ride was swell. From Timashore it only took twelve hours. The train was a big, fast one. We didn't get a Pullman, but we had the next best thing.

We did have to wait in the station for about 2 hours before anyone came to tell us what to do. Finally, a full colonel came with his eagle on a Russian Cossak hat. He had a couple of trucks and a bus and took us to the mission in a French nun's hospital. Got good food and a bath and clean clothes and delousing.

3-17-45

The nuns and American personnel here treat us fine. The doc, a major, is in charge of us. He is very insistent that we got to sick call.

Here the boys got the first cigarette for days. They'd been smoking home spun tobacco rolled in newspaper on the train. We're told our families will know we are ok in 48 hrs. I know this is most likely not true but feel better about it. We can go to town tomorrow, but must be back at 6:00 PM. There is often shooting and trouble in town at nite.

3-18-45

They have lots of stuff here that we can't get at the base. Wish we had more money. They have American shows here. Saw Dick Powell and Myrna Loy this afternoon.

All the young men and many of the women from this place have been taken by the war. The result is that the remaining women are very eager to have fun with the Americans. Their aim being to grab as much fun as they can while they can. We had church tonite in the mission.

3-19-45

They say we might leave tomorrow or next day, so we're spending all the Lei we have so we won't leave with a lot of money we can't get lire for. I bought a bunch of cigarette lighters, and some cheap mantle pieces.

If I had more money, I could get a German pistol or some nice blouses for my sisters. Trouble is I'd have to get so many blouses. I'd like to leave and get back so I could write home.

3-20-45

We all got our stuff ready and went out to the airport in busses at noon. Stood around for an hour or so then came back and went to town. The Russians won't clear any ships before March 22.

Didn't do much in town except go to the show. I'm about out of money.

3-21-45

Today I sneaked out six panels of parachute and sold it. Got about the equivalent of thirteen bucks for it. Bought a P 38 German pistol for six bucks. That leaves me seven to go on.

Cy and Jim slept out tonite.

3-22-45

Today at noon we took off in a C 47 for Bari. Had an uneventful trip. Took about 3 ½ hours.

We went to the 22 replacement depot and got a bath and a new issue of clothes. Slept in a tent in an apple orchard in full bloom, nearly froze.

3-23-45

Got interegated at AF Headquarters this morning and met Major Charlton at the airport at noon. He flew us back to the base. It's wonderful to be back.

I have 45 accumulated letters. Maggie took good care of our stuff tho he couldn't keep them from moving it out. He also wrote Mother and I'm sure made it easier on her.

3-24-45

Spent the day reading mail and getting moved back in the tent.

Everyone seems fine at home. Also everyone here seems glad to see us back and think we should be sent home.

3-25-45

Went to church this morning. Also to sick call. Have a hell of a cold.

3-26-45

Today we all saw the Flight Surgeon. He is deciding what to do with us. Grounded Hahn and Bugg because of their nerves. I doubt if they'll get to go home right away tho. The rest of us are to fly a couple of sorties then to the rest camp.

3-27-45

Cy was supposed to fly with Summerhays today in a lead ship to get checked out as a box leader. They had a standown tho. Looks like the month is going out "like a lion."

3-28-45

We were scheduled to fly today, but got a standown because of the weather. Played poker and read instead. We'll be scheduled again tomorrow.

The war news of late is wonderful. The West front is moving east so rapidly they can't keep track of it. The atmosphere around here is about a thousand percent lighter because of this news.

3-29-45

Another standown today. Guess the weather up north is really bad. It isn't so good here.

Cy and I went to the line today and I shot landings from the left seat. They say they want him to get checked out as box leader and me to take the crew between the times he flies. I was quite pleased with the landings.

3-30-45

Standown again today. Just read and played poker all day. No mail.

3-31-45

Were briefed for Linz today. The group bombed Villach tho. I'm pretty disgusted.

We lost two generators after takeoff and had to land and get one of them fixed, then took off and caught the formation. They flew thru a lot of weather up over the north Adriatic and we lost the formation and early returned.

April 1945

4-1-45

We were briefed for two plans today. Linz was one and Bruck the other. Much to our relief, they decided to hit Bruck which is only 10 or 15 miles ahead of a Russian spearhead.

We got weather again over the target and the whole group returned. For some reason we got credit for the sorties. We were all surprised at that.

4-2-45

Nothing today. Flew the link trainer for two hrs this afternoon. Went to see a show this evening. "Sweet and Low Down" with Benny Goodman and his orchestra.

4-3-45

We were supposed to lead a practice mission of six ships this afternoon. As we taxied out to take off the left tire blew out. We were sure glad it was on the taxi way instead of on the takeoff landing.

We returned to the tent and laid around the rest of the day.

4-4-45

We flew the practice mission this afternoon. Took five ships down to the heel of the boot and camera bombed the rail yards at a town called Leece. It wasn't a bad trip and only took a couple of hours.

Seems like everyone on the base is drunk tonite. Didn't get to sleep till 2:00 AM.

4-5-45

Slept till 11:00 AM today. We had a formation at 1:00 to present DFC's to three boys. This C. S. Major we have for C. O. took a Cpl and fined a Lt $75 today because the Cpl failed to salute the Lt and the Lt didn't call him down. Everyone is pretty sore about it. We don't feel we should have to salute in combat. We never have till now. Guess they think the war is over.

We're scheduled to fly tomorrow.

4-6-45

Flew a dry run today. Were briefed to go to northern Italy but they called off the mission because of bad weather shortly after takeoff. We had to fly around till noon in order to burn up some of the gas load so we could safely land with the bombs.

Just laid around and slept and read. No mail for three days.

4-7-45

We were briefed to bomb a bridge in the Brenner pass, intense flak, but had to return with the bombs because the target was cloud covered and they don't allow radar work in that area.

We got moderate and very accurate flak on the way back over the Italian Riviera. Seems you can't cross there anymore without getting shot at. This was about as hard a mission as I've had. The ship seemed to be losing two engines on one side all the way.

4-8-45.

Went to church this morning and to a news cast this afternoon. Wrote letters and read the rest of the day. We're up to fly again tomorrow.

4-9-45

We've had a lot of excitement about this mission today. Had a general here etc. We went to northern Italy and bombed the front lines about a mile from the British 8th [Army]. They had all sorts of arrows and stuff on the ground pointing at the target and shot flak up under us to mark the front lines. Saw scant flak, was a good mission.

4-10-45

Did exactly the same thing as yesterday except bombed about a mile farther on. Followed the same arrows and smoke pots into the target. Flak was much worse today. The 46th lost a ship over the target.

4-11-45

Did nothing today except read and take a sunbath. Had a late letter from the folks tonite.

4-12-45

We had a practice mission today on the gunnery range. Rather enjoyed it. The range is a section of barren coast down in the arch of the boot. They have dummy airplanes, etc on the ground to shoot. We fly along at 100 to 200 feet above the ground and the gunners in the turrets shoot, then we make a wide pattern out over the water and go around for another run.

Took it easy this afternoon.

4-13-45

Got news of F. D. R.'s death today. Just laid around and read.

Went to the show. Saw "Rapsody in Blue." A little more classical music than I wanted to listen to.

4-14-45

Had a baseball game this afternoon. Rather enjoyed it. Got letters from home.

4-15-45

Today I took the crew on the mission as first pilot, for the first time. Cy flew with a box leader. He's getting checked out as leader.

I had another boy who's been flying co-pilot almost as long as I have. Got along fine. We dropped 100 lb clusters on German troops and gun emplacements ahead of the 5th army just south of Boloria [Bologna?], Italy. Not so much flak, but it was pretty accurate. These short missions are better.

Had an electrical fire in the navigator's compartment on the way back that scared us a bit but got it out ok after it burnt up a lot of radar equipment. Maggie also had to de-fuse and tie to the racks (with wire electrical cords etc.) two bombs that wouldn't fall out for us.

4-16-45

Test hopped a ship with Haymond today. That's about all.

No mail tonite. Maggie flew with another crew today.

4-17-45

Bombed in support of the 5th army today. I flew with Cy. Had about a dozen bursts of flak in or near the box. There wasn't much but it was very close.

Flew over Rome and also saw a tower in a town called Pizza. There seems to be a question as to whether it is the leaning tower or not. All considered it was a good mission.

4-18-45

I planned to go to Bari today but woke up to find myself scheduled for a practice formation mission. It was not bad. I flew as Pilot and got Joe Bitts for Co-pilot.

We went to Naples, out over the Isle of Capri, to the heel of Italy and then back. Looks like we will all get lots of practice missions from now on.

Now I'm too lazy to go to Bari tomorrow, as I'll probably have to fly the next day.

4-19-45

Nothing much doing. I read Wendell Wilkie's "One World."

Cy went to the hospital yesterday with a bad cold and cough. Rabbit flew today and Maggie and I just laid around.

4-20-45

I flew co-pilot for Capt Koile in Able 2. Had a good ship and a good mission. Hit a bridge on a secondary road, across the first river north of the Poe over which the Germans are evacuating troops. Used 1000 lb bombs. There were beautiful hits on several bridges along this river. I've never seen so many bombs so well placed. There was a lot of flak off to our right, but we luckily got none of it.

Cy is still in the hospital here on the base.

4-21-45

Nothing today. Just being around. Had an inspection this morning but I missed it by feigning a practice mission. Went to the line and returned during inspection. Maggie flew. Reports good mission.

4-22-45

Went to church this morning and finished a book I started yesterday this afternoon.

4-23-45

Went to Bari today and had a very pleasant time. Got a bunch of pictures I've taken with my new camera printed. Developed them myself the other nite with borrowed equipment.

Took in a show, got some shows at the PX too. Spring is here, but I damn near froze to death on the truck coming back.

Maggie and Rabbit flew. Got a little flak.

4-24-45

Nothing today. Started to read "Inside Europe." Had a talk with Major Charlton this evening and got permission to go to Bari for a couple of days.

I haven't been scheduled to fly for four days now. Seems they are trying to finish up all the boys they can in a hurry. Everyone seems to think we'll go non-operational very soon. I don't think I'll be able to finish.

4-25-45

Bari today.

4-26-45

Bari again.

4-27-45

Same

4-28-45

Hitchhiked back to the base this afternoon. It was a very pleasant trip. The road is lined with blooming locusts which are very fragrant.

Not much doing while I was gone. The Sqdn lost one crew over Linz. I find we've orders to go to Capri on rest leave the 30th.

I'm scheduled to fly a practice mission.

4-29-45

Went to church tonite. I flew co-pilot for Kaas on a blue bomb mission to Pianosa, an Island in the Adriatic. It was routine, nothing exciting.

We are getting in seventeen new officers who have 25 to 30 sorties from the 485th B. X. which is going thru the states to the Pacific. These boys are supposed to finish with us. I don't see how they will.

We are not flying much if any these last few days. We have decided to move into a house with

Summerhay's crew. It's too big. We'll pay him $25 each.

4-30-45

Got up early and went to the finance office and drew part pay of $100. Came back and threw some stuff in a bag and we took off for Naples about 9:30 AM. It was beautiful out at the Naples airport. They have a lot of beautiful P-61's and some British stuff.

We went to Naples and spent an hour or two there. Seems to be lots of fun to be had. Crossed over to Capri on a steamer. Took about two hours. Then we came up the side of a rock cliff on a finapuli [funicular].

Hotel, beds, food are swell. Dance that nite at hotel.

May 1945

5-1-45

The place [Capri] is different from anywhere I've ever been. The town is in a notch in the sheer rock which goes on up above and down below. There's a gap, however, so you can see the water on both sides of the island. Some of the streets are wide enough to get a Jeep thru and others aren't. There are many beautiful souvineers.

Took a horse drawn taxi to another town that's on the very top of a pinnacle. The road goes up the side of the rock cliff. This afternoon at the hotel they had a concert, which was very good, and a May pole dance.

5-2-45

Rained today. We just laid around the hotel and took life easy. Cy and Maggie were sick last night. Too much coniac.

They had a dance tonite at a place very appropriately called the Booby Trap. It is just a basement with a bar and a brassy band.

We had our caricature drawn this afternoon. Wrote Mother.

5-3-45

We took a motor boat around the island. The sun was out, but the sea was very rough. We all got soaking wet form the salt spray.

Saw the white grotto, but the water is too rough to go in the blue grotto today. The white one is above the water level and you walk in it thru a series of tunnels. It is a large hole full of geographic formations, from which you can look out to the sea.

I just wandered around town this afternoon. Tonite they had a radio show in the theater. It was very good.

5-4-45

It's a beautiful day. Loafed around town this morning and picked up a few of the less expensive souvenirs. Maggie paid $120 for an unmounted cameo. It's beautiful. Guess it should be.

Cy, Maggie, and I started to the Blue Grotto in some kayaks we rented but didn't quite make it. Mine and Maggie's got full of water before we got there and we had to give up the trip. A British motor launch picked me up, but Cy and Maggie made it under their own power.

5-5-45

Walked up to Tiberius Caesar's ruins this morning. Enjoyed it immensely, he certainly must have had a beautiful and expensive place there. It commands the best views of anywhere I've ever been. He had many women brought up there, one for every day of the week and several spares. If one did not please him or got pregnant, he threw her over the cliff.

This afternoon I went to the Blue Grotto in a sail boat. It's indeed beautiful, I also enjoyed the trip there very much. We're having a dance tonite.

5-6-45

Cy and I returned to Naples this morning. Maggie and Rabbit will come tomorrow. The trip across was rather pleasant. We loafed around town today and just looked it over.

Tonite I went with the boys to a place to drink and dance. Got bored and came home early. Naples is very nice. You see lots of pretty girls. The harbor is still full of capsized ships.

5-7-45

We slept late this morning; then caught a truck out to the field at noon. Had to lie around there till 5:00 PM before we took off. The ship we were to fly home in blew an air duct. We luckily caught a 464th [Bomb Group] ship home.

Everything here is fine. The war is over and it looks like we will go home. Have lots of mail.

5-8-45

Beautiful day today. I went to Naples with some boys who are going home this morning just more or less to be sure I get my flying time in. It was a nice trip.

This afternoon Jake got a Jeep and Cive [Milakovic?], Cy, and I went with him to Barletta and another town over on the Adriatic swimming. Had a good time and took some pictures.

Cy and I moved in with Hook and Jake tonite. It is much better than the hot, dirty tent.

5-9-45

Did nothing except start reading "The Robe" and moved a little more of my stuff down here. Paid Hook $25 for the privilege of moving in. It is certainly 10 times better than the tent.

5-10-45

Rumor has it that we're to go to Trinidad to fly one leg of the route the 5th army is to be flown home [on]. Have done nothing today.

5-11-45

Nothing today. Lots of rumors about going home.

5-12-45

Cy got scheduled to fly some instruments today. I did exactly nothing, just read.

5-13-45

I was scheduled to fly instruments today with Badycomb, and Balmont. We flew over to Naples and looked down in the big hole in the top of Mt. Vesuvius, then up and looked Rome over, then back over Capri and home. I did fly the beam home from Naples and made an approach. We all shot landings.

Went to church tonite.

5-14-45

Packed my winter things and some stuff I got in Bucharest and Capri in a box and sent it to Mother.

Filled out a personal affairs form and got my flying equipment checked. It looks like we will be flying to the states pretty soon. I'm happy, but not as much so as I thought I'd be. Worrying about the Pacific.

5-15-45

Went over to the finance office in the major's Jeep and drew a $100 partial pay this morning. We got some more poop on going home this evening. Seems we're to go in a truck to Goia [Gioia], the place we came to from Tunis, and pick up a ship to fly to the states from there. Guess we will leave pretty soon. We are alerted and can leave the post. My promotion came thru today. Seems I'm now a 1st Lt.

5-16-45

Walked down to the river to swim and shoot my German pistol. Rather enjoyed it, but it's too far to walk. Not much doing.

5-17-45

Maggie and Rabbit moved down to the house today. We took all the wood out of the tent and have it all ready to take down.

I drew officer of the day today. Did not have much to do except mount guard and close the enlisted mens and officers bar. It's a no good job.

5-18-45

Not much doing around here. The boys are flying kites just to pass the time. We're all getting pretty restless. We're having revile and formation twice a day for roll call now. Have to get up at 6:00 AM just to start sitting around. It's a rough war.

5-19-45

Nothing today. I'm reading "Forever Amber." Very filthy and obscene.

We're getting very restless and would like to do, or at least know something definite. Steve, one of the boys we knew at Tucson, came over to see Cy today. He's a Captain now. Most of the boys we know are either home or went down.

5-20-45

Went to church this morning in the new chapel. It's the first Sunday since they finished building it. It's a surprisingly fine chapel, for materials are very scarce here. They fired all the Italian workers and the enlisted men are doing KP for us. They are quite bitter.

5-21-45

The boys who are flying from here to Goia [Gioia] are loading their baggage in the ships today. It's rumored they are to leave tomorrow and go to another place and go to Goia [Gioia] later. Guess we'll go in three days or so. No, we're to leave tomorrow also, they say, via truck.

They're having us make final preparations for leaving. Burnt all our furniture and packed everything. All the tents have been taken down and it looks like rain. Glad we're in a house.

5-22-45

We're all ready for an 8:30 AM takeoff for Manderia [Manduria] tomorrow. We're not too eager about Manderia [Manduria] or the flight there.

They're loading two crews and baggage in one ship. That's too much with all the baggage we have. I'm afraid we'll get stuck there for a while and that it will be a bad place.

5-23-45

The flight today went as scheduled and the whole group arrived ok.

Seems I guessed about right about Manderia [Manduria] being a bad deal. We have a hut to live in ok, but there are many flies and the food is the worst ever.

Seems we will be here at least ten days, then go to Goia [Gioia] for processing. It would have been better to have stayed at the base and gone directly to Goia [Gioia]. My atheletes foot is giving me the first real trouble since high school days.

5-24-45

My feet were so sore this morning I could hardly walk. Had to go on sick call. The Dr and all the medics are negroes. They fixed me up fine, tho, and my feet are better tonite.

We're not doing a thing here but waiting for them to get room to take us to Goia [Gioia]. Looks like we will be here ten days or two weeks.

Maggie went to Bari and got some magazines. Bari is about 90 miles north. We went to a show in an open air theater last nite and tonite.

5-25-45

Just laying around reading. Food here is terrible.

5-26-45

Same. Got some PX rations this evening. Saw Hedy Lamarr at the show.

5-27-45

Nothing today. Some of the boys are picking over some old planes here that are to be assigned to us to fly home. There are none here, however, that look safe to start across all that water with. I think we won't sign up to fly one if we can help it at all. If we can't get a better one at Goia [Gioia], I'd rather go home on a boat.

5-28-45

Looks like we will definitely have to fly one of these ships home. Some of the boys are coming back from Goia [Gioia] to pick up these. They say the ones there are worse.

I got to talking to a big black sgt who is more or less in charge of the ships and found an old one with less than 200 hours on it. It has belonged to the R. A. F. and seems to be in fine shape. We signed up for it. Will know more about it if we test hop it tomorrow. No, we flew it today and it seems ok.

5-29-45

Flew the ship yesterday. Rabbit swung the compass while we checked the ship. Seems ok.

Today I laid around all morning and caught the mail truck to Bari. Went thru Taranto, which looks like a better town than Bari. I had a very pleasant trip up and left some film with my photographer friend, went to a USO dance, etc. Slept with the same family I stayed with last time I was here.

5-30-45

Loafed at the photographer's a while this morning and took in a show "For Whom The Bell Tolls." Came out of the show and it was raining very hard. I luckily had a bag with a suit of [Army] greens in it with me. I stepped inside a doorway and took off my suntans and put on the greens and got them soaking while walking to meet the truck. Changed back and had a good trip back.

Cy is in town tonite and there is nothing new here.

Map showing location in Italy's "heel." Point A is Manduria.
Taranto is on the way to Bari (point B), on the coast.

5-31-45

Cy is still in Taranto. I attended a pilots' meeting for him today.

They are going to give us a pre-processing here before we go to Goia [Gioia]. We will probably get ours tomorrow or the next day.

Guess we won't get paid again this month. Reason is still because they haven't heard from Washington on that last m.i.a. I've only drawn $200 in partials in the last three months. Guess I'll have between five and six hundred bucks coming now. Have over $150 in my pocket.

June 1945

6-1-45

We had another meeting today and were told we must pull a 100 hr inspection on our ships ourselves. It will be quite a job. We pulled all the cowlings this afternoon and found that most of all of the hoses in the ship are bad, gas and hydraulic, and oil lines. Also most of the rubber air duct gaskets are rotten. We haven't decided whether we should try and replace the worst of it, an almost hopeless job, or turn the ship back in, which would no doubt delay going home.

6-2-45

Decided to let them have the ship back. Now we have no ship and will probably be here longer. Don't know how much. I let Cy and the boys put the cowling back on this morning and I read. They had quite a time with it.

Many of our boys are scheduled to leave tomorrow, including the crew Maggie is flying with. Sure hate to see him go. He's been swell to live with. We played hearts this afternoon and watched the ball game this eve.

6-3-45

Nothing new except more of the crews are leaving. There will only be a few left if the ones scheduled to go tomorrow leave. We'd be going tomorrow if we hadn't fooled with the airplane.

We went down to the beach today past Manderia [Manduria]. I don't like salt water. Maggie left today. Sure miss the old boy. It's the first time we've been away from him for eleven months, except the last m.i.a. Hope to see him again.

6-4-45

Nothing much today except Hook, Jake, and Red left us. We're scheduled to go Wednesday.

The food here is atrocious. I'm enjoying just laying around dreaming of going home. Guess I'll run into Taranto tomorrow. I have a few cigarettes to dispose of.

Just left the show early. No good and I'd seen it before.

6-5-45

Went to Bari today and had a fairly pleasant trip. Just myself and the driver.

I got back at 6:00 PM to find that another change had been made in our status. We now have been assigned another klunker to fly home. Cy and Monty have it all ready to go. Swing the compass, etc. tomorrow. The show was better tonite.

6-6-45

We flew the ship for two hours this morning. It's older and worse in my opinion than the one we had before. We're pulling another 100 hr inspection on it tho so I guess it will be ok.

We're scheduled on the board to leave tomorrow but that's impossible because there is another day's work on the ship.

I'm reading "The Sun Is My Undoing." It's pretty good. Saw a sordid show tonite.

6-7-45

The boys are working on the ship. I was able to get a colored mechanic to do some of the work and supervise them. I've been out there a couple or three times, but have been staying pretty much out of their way. I'm sure it isn't best to stand over them. Cy doesn't see it that way. They think the ship is ready to go as soon as we get some oil.

We're supposed to go tomorrow. It'll be good to get away from here. USO show tonite.

6-8-45

The oil truck came after we'd gotten our stuff out to the ship and gotten it loaded. We started to go but found that we had two fuel pressures much too high. Had to stop the engines and get the colored boy again. He set back one of them but had to change another fuel pump.

We ate lunch over at Hq. mess (swanky outfit) and finally got off about 2:30 PM. Flew up to Goia [Gioia] in about 30 min. They say we'll fly this ship and will probably be here three days.

Slept in tents. Food is better.

6-9-45

There are 1000 ships here, I guess. The place has grown and improved considerably since we were here on the way over. They told Cy he would have to fly this ship back and he apparently accepted that without a question. I'm rather bitter at him for not at least trying to get another. They have plenty of new ones here. I'm sure I would not be so easy to get along with were I in his position. The life of a co-pilot is not a pleasant one.

I read most of the day. We may process tomorrow.

6-10-45

We aren't processing today. I read literally all day. Am about half thru "The Sun Is My Undoing." It has over 1000 pages and is pretty good.

They say we will process tomorrow and leave the next day. Most of the ships leaving today and tomorrow are B 17's.

I wrote John a note today. Am getting a bit restless to get away and started home. We have with us now a Capt and a 1st Lt P-38 Pilot who are going home with us as passengers.

6-11-45

Things seem to be moving in the right direction at last. We got processed today quite efficiently after they got started, and loaded our baggage on the ship tonite. We are to take off at 8:00 AM tomorrow for Merriketch [Marrakech]. The weather looks sorta messy now, first time for days, but it may pass by morning. If the ship will just keep going we'll be ok.

The passengers seem to be pretty good boys. Got our Lire changed to greenbacks.

6-12-45

Finally got away after much adoo. Had electrical trouble in the ship and spent the nite and morning up to and after takeoff time getting it fixed. Fuel transfer pump wouldn't work.

I was indeed sweating the old klunker out till we got across the Mediterranean, then I'd just gotten east over Algiers when we discovered gas pouring from a valve in the bomb bay. We started to land there but finally got the leak slowed up and came on. The heat here is terrible. 100 degrees in the shade.

6-13-45

This place has improved greatly since we came thru here nine months ago. The food is swell tho you do pay for it, and they have a bar with cokes and juices, which is quite a treat after not having any for so long.

They found three leaky valves instead of one and sent to Casablanca for them. We thought we would get off this morning but they didn't get the valves fixed. Were briefed the Azores route, which is very much better than via Dakar and Natel.

6-14-45

We went to town yesterday afternoon. There's not much doing tho it was pleasant just to look at the French girls. They finally got fuel valves last nite and are fixing the ship. We thought it would be done this morning and went to a lot of trouble to see Colonels, etc. and get on the Azores route again.

It is a very hard deal to pull and I'm just hoping we have not bothered them so much they won't put us on again tomorrow. It's two days shorter that way.

6-15-45

The fact that we have such a klunker to fly got us on the Azores route. We were very happy to get to go this way. We got off at 7:20 this morning and had a good trip. Arrived here at 1:10.

Had a broken undercast all the way. Let down thru a hole about 50 mi out. It's very crowded here. Twelve of us are in a tent. The PX and mess are wonderful tho. Just like the states. Very hard to get used to. Most of the boys here are 8th AF boys and have had an easy life. We are to brief at 1:00 AM.

6-16-45

They woke us up at 4:00 AM for a 6:00 briefing but called it off because of weather at Gander. Maybe we'll get off tomorrow.

We're just lying around today. May take in a show this afternoon.

I went to the ship this morning and got my sheet and air mattress. Was very uncomfortable last night. This island base is really a treat after Italy. They have cokes, ice cream, juke boxes, the latest magazines, etc. Also they use American money.

6-17-45

They woke us up at 2:00 this morning and briefed us at 4:00. We were to take off at 6:30 AM but when we tried to start the engines we found the batteries were completely dead and the "put put" and one generator were out. We thought maybe we could get rid of this old wreck and go home on a C

54 so we wrote everything we could find wrong with it, but they're fixing it today so we'll take off tomorrow, weather permitting. We're sleeping today.

6-18-45

The weather was bad today and no one took off. We went down to test hop the ship this afternoon and found a big, long crack in a supercharger. We didn't fly it and they're changing superchargers tonite. We may get off tomorrow but I doubt it.

I wrote Mother a note today. Guess she's wondering about me by now. Went to the gym and heard the post band play some popular music tonite. They are very good.

Hope we get out of here soon. I'd like to get home.

6-19-45

They changed the supercharger last nite and we test hopped the ship this afternoon. It seems to be ok. Hope it will get us home now. The weather map looks very bad. I doubt if we'll get off tomorrow either. At least we are ready to take off when the weather gets good enough.

We're all very restless and anxious to get home.

6-20-45

Nothing much doing today. It's fairly pleasant to read and listen to records in the officers club. Also we get all the goods and sweets we want here which is a welcome change.

The weather map still looks bad. They say we have a 50/50 chance to get off in the morning. The winds are down to about 25 MPH headwind. Sure hope we go.

6-21-45

Well, we didn't get off again today and chances look very poor for tomorrow. This is getting indeed monotonous.

I mailed a note to Jeanne this morning. Hope I at least beat it home. 1st Lt Doss, one of our passengers, found today that he has the scabies. They took all our blankets away to de-louse them.

Damn, we're getting tired of this. I believe we'd take off with a 50 MPH head wind if they'd let us.

6-22-45

They awoke us for briefing very unexpectedly this morning and we got here at least and ok. I'm the happiest I've been in a long time tonite. I've really been dreading that long over water hop in that old wreck. The ship is a mess. If we had had good sense we would have flatly refused to take it. There's something wrong with No 2 engine. The prop vibrates too badly.

We had another gas leak way out over that cold water today. Guess it will take them a day or so to fix it. We go from here to the states and a 30 day leave. Flew from Azores to Gander in 9 hrs 10 min.

I flew 1 ½ hours of actual instruments. Got a good bit of ice on the ship.

<u>6-23-45</u>

Got back to the states today, Bradley field, Conn. It's really wonderful, can't get used to it. We took off in very bad weather and flew thru a lot worse.

They've been processing us this evening and tonite. I'm very, very tired. We're to get up and go on a train to camp Miles Standish tomorrow.

I sent Mother and Jeanne a wire this evening.

6-24-45

We were hauled to the train on trucks this morning and reached this place at noon. Had a rather pleasant ride.

I was very impressed by all the people along the way waving at us. Many of them were here 24 to 48 hrs. Food is good.

I called Dad today. He says everyone is fine but they're all at Welch. I'd sorta hoped some of them would be at Morgantown.

6-25-45

This is a pretty good post, but it's sorta barren and sandy, which was a bit of a surprise to me. Haven't done anything at all note-worthy today. Read, tried to call Frances, checked on some war Dept circulars at Hq etc.

I'm very anxious to get home and also quite uneasy about my next assignment. My conscience will let me stay in the states if the army will. We are to leave in the morning.

6-26-45

Said "Good-By" to Cy and all the boys today and am alone tonite.

Thus, Charles A. "Chuck" Haynes ended his recollections as a B-24 Bomber co-pilot; just as he started, *alone*. He began as a "scared kid," thrust into a job he had never anticipated or imagined, and ended his tour of duty as a combat forged, seasoned aviator.

Nevertheless, his farewell to Curtis I. "Cy" Eatman, didn't end their friendship; a friendship strengthened and deepened by shared combat experience into a relationship akin to brothers, if not by birth, by love. They remained close friends until Curtis's death.

After the death of his wife Kathryn, Charles courted and eventually married Curtis's widow, Betty, continuing their close friendship even after his death. Charles and Betty enjoyed a long and loving union until Betty went to be with her first husband. Not long after, Charles followed them.

World War II engulfed the entire globe in a contest of fascism versus freedom, providing a rich panoply of stories that will fascinate and occupy historians for decades to come. Yet, upon that greater stage, individuals like Charles A. Haynes strode and told their own unique stories.

At such a time, the performers aren't always "great men," as we have come to think of them, but

From the Farm to the Cockpit

millions of "everymen" who, though formerly unknown to the world at large, nevertheless play their own part in the greater story.

Charles A. Haynes, a farm boy from Morgantown, West Virginia, not only played his part but had the foresight to write about it. "I, the co-pilot, decided that before I went to sleep that night I would jot down a few notes relative to the day's happenings. My diary is the result...." This simple decision preserved his thoughts, his impressions and his feelings for posterity to experience decades later.

In his simple and straightforward manner, he bequeathed, not merely a dry retelling of a great historical event, but a very *human* story we can all relate to.

In that telling, far past his death, he has become, in his own way, immortal.

Appendix I

Minutes:

March 3, 1945, Pécs (Hungary)

The following minutes were taken by the Commission which was composed of the following: Chairman of the Commission, the Military Commandant of the City of Pécs, Major Savon. Members: Adjutant to the Commandant of the City of Pécs, 1st Lt. Warkan, and the authorized 17 VA Engineer A.E. Technical Lt. Kolupanko.

The following minutes were taken on the matter:

On the 4th of March, 1945, a forced landing was made on the airfield of the City of Pécs by the American airplane B-24 No. 904 of the 15 (th) American Air Corps of 465 Bombardier Group. Upon examination it was found:

1. In the first motor on the left side, the cylinder was cracked.

2. The middle motor on the right (of series) was frozen. Major damage was found in the cylinder. The cause of the damage in the body of the motor appears to be the lack of oil.

Conclusion:

Airplane B-24 No. 904 is unfit for further action. Two new motors are needed for the repair of the airplane. The personnel of the airplane consists of ten men:

1. 1st Lt. Curtis I. Eatman
2. 2nd Lt. Charles A. Haynes
3. 1st Lt. Raymond Milakovic
4. F. O. William E. Evans
5. T/Sgt Lamont H. Pakes

6. T/Sgt James Powerll
7. S/Sgt Edward W. Hahn
8. S/Sgt James E. Stephen
9. S/Sgt James T. Bugg
10. T/Sgt William E. Alvey

March 6, 1945 they were sent by auto transport escorted by Capt. Novechkov for disposal by the head of the 3rd Ukrainian fronts, Major Gen. Pavlov. All personal equipment and parachutes were sent away with the fliers.

Commission:

Military Commandant of the City of Pécs: Major Savon

Adjutant of the Military Commandant: 1st Lt. Norken

Authorized by 17 V A: 1st Technician Lt. Kolupanko

The Commandant of Personnel: Curtis I. Eatman

Appendix II

[Note: What follows is some first-person, post-war descriptive information by Chuck Haynes recalling his experiences during WW II. – T. H. Pine]

1st Short Discussion About B-24's
Part of our Part of WW II

I hadn't seen much direct publicity given to this subject over the ensuing years, until very recently when Senator McGovern's experiences were published in book form and condensed in a national magazine. It is real amazing to me to see the similarity in his and our experiences, recorded in my diary of so many years ago.

Pantanella Air Base at which we were stationed was only a very few miles from his Spinizola Base. They were both near Foggia, Italy which was located some maybe sixty miles north of Bari, a fairly large town on Italy's east coast of the Adriatic Sea.

Most all missions from these and several other bases in the area headed on a course diagonally across the Adriatic Sea in a north easterly direction to landfall on the northwest portion of Yugoslavia. From there they would mostly fan out in the direction of their assigned target areas.

Some of the more dangerous targets as far as flak goes were sites of railroad yards and petroleum refineries. Some of the names of those which struck fear in the minds of the crews were Munich, Lenz, Blechammer, North and Blechammer, South, Vienna, Austria on the banks of the "Beautiful Blue Danube," mostly the muddy Danube in the winter months.

I used the word "flak" a couple of sentences ago. This word "flak" may need an explanation. Flak were steel encased explosives which when fired from the ground were armed to explode at the location of the bombing aircraft. When the explosion occurred, the steel casing became flying razor sharp pieces of metal which were invisible and a puff of black smoke which was very visible. A direct hit of an aircraft would and did demolish the aircraft, and its contents.

Most targets would be bombed from an altitude of 18 or 20,000 feet by a fleet of 50 or 100 (more or less) planes. That many planes in formation (which was necessary for fighter protection) gave the ground gunners a very large target at which to direct their flak. Most enemy action encountered by us involved flak. By the time we arrived, the fighter planes had been eliminated by others. When the Air Force assigned Lt. Curtis Eatman's crew, a co-pilot named Charles Haynes neither apparently cared for the other's first name. As a result, the co-pilot became "Chuck" and the pilot "CI," his initials, later changed to Cy. This occurred in 1944.

As the aircraft assigned to Lt. Eatman for delivery to the 15th Air Force at Pantanella Air Base near Foggia, Italy flew from Topeka, Kansas to Manchester New Hampshire, I, the co-pilot, decided that before I went to sleep that night I would jot down a few notes relative to the day's happenings. My diary is the result, certainly no literary work, just the daily musings of a scared kid forced by circumstances into a man's job. Most of the diary consists of calendar days on which nothing of interest happened. It also includes several days on which events were very life threatening.

From the Farm to the Cockpit

Shortly after arrival at Pantanella Bomber Base, Foggia, Ialy, indoctrination lectures did not paint any nice pictures. Among other statistics quoted by the Maintenance Division Captain, he said they had an excellent record of keeping the aircraft flying. They only lost 5% of their aircraft due to maintenance problems. Returning from the lecture, I asked Cy what he thought about the 5% loss. We agreed that, somewhere about 20 missions of the 100 we were then expected to fly before rotation to the states, we would be downed due to faulty maintenance. We didn't sleep well that night.

On Dec. 18, 1944, our group, with others, bombed Blechhammer North Oil Refinery, 700 miles north of our base. Our crew was assigned one of the oldest aircraft in our squadron and it performed accordingly. We lost #3 engine for all practical purposes on the way to the target, completely lost

#4 over the target to flak and the supercharger on #2 shortly after the target.

After the remaining main body of the right [box] left the target area for home base, several stragglers including us were left behind and vulnerable to enemy fighters. The stragglers were soon alone, having lost each other due to different speeds and altitudes. Tail winds gave us a remote possibility to reach an emergency airport on the island of Vis in the harbor of Split, Yugoslavia. This, a little later, failed due to cloud coverage, competing traffic, and a further loss of engine power. Cy then concluded our only option was the "bail out" over the mountains in Yugoslavia. The sighting of Split harbor through an isolated break in the cloud coverage, indicating a heading of 30 degrees for approximately five minutes, gave us the opportunity to do the bail out and gave us a position fix over the mountains. A bail out over the cold and lonely Adriatic was not recommended, or desirable.

Our pre-flight briefings constantly reminded us that Yougo military forces consisted of three groups: Tito's Partisians, who could be expected to attempt to get you back to your base, The Chetnichs, who might help or hurt you, and The Ustache, who would cut your throats.

We did bail out one at a time with Magee, the bombardier in charge of getting all the enlisted personnel and the Navigator out. After reporting to Cy that all were safely out, he said, "Good Bye for now," and I also left. Cy insisted that I go before him and I was able to see him come out of the plane and his chute open. I did call to him but did not hear him answer. He later said he'd heard me and did answer. He landed in a barnyard and I on top of a mountain with my chute hung [up] in the lower branches of a big pine tree. I hit the ground harder than I expected and I think maybe the deep snow helped lessen the contact.

Later in the day, he and I got together in a farm house where he had landed. I found him inside with a very large family, with maybe 6 or 8 adults and a few children. Also in the house, but in another room, were some cows and calves. The folks and Cy were lying around on straw on the floor. Cy said we should not offend the people by refusing to eat from a family bowl of what looked to be curdled milk. We tried. It was a long afternoon and night.

We found, much to our relief, that when the soldiers came in the morning they wore the red star on their uniforms indicating affiliation with Tito's Partisans. We were to accompany them to find the rest of our crew and eventually [get] back to our base. This information came very hard as they did not speak our language, nor us theirs. Also, we did not know that they had heard from others at least rumors that the rest of us were okay, except for a couple of broken legs.

With their help we found the other crew members over the next two or three days. Two of them did have broken legs, which were splinted with broken tree limbs, and the men placed on mules. Some days later, we left the two injured at a small hospital for medical attention.

When we were assured the injured had preceded us, we boarded a freight car on a narrow gauge railway for the start of our trip back to base. Our Christmas dinner was a portion of one small can of corned beef shared by four of us and furnished by the Partisans.

The trip back to our base was relatively uneventful. We arrived at our tent site, (the tent and our belongings having been removed during our absence) late December 30.

Russian Lines

On March 4, 1945, on a normal approach to a target with a sick airplane which got sicker by starting to lose supercharges, we were unable to maintain air speed and altitude to stay with our flight, so we aborted the bombing run. We continued to lose altitude and dropped our bombs in an effort to stay with the Group, which was unsuccessful. During our decent we lost #3 engine completely, along with the troublesome superchargers on #2 & #4 engines.

Having been briefed before the mission, as was the custom, on several possible landing sites in the area of the path to the target, Cy selected a fighter strip at Pécs, Hungary as our preferred alternate.

Finding the strip became somewhat of a challenge as we had all become quite disoriented during our efforts to remain with the group. We did find it and reached it with enough altitude to make a standard approach pattern for the runway.

The approach end of the runway did have a low fence across it and the runway terminated at the other end just before becoming the main street of the small town of Pécs. Cy did a beautiful job of putting the plane across the fence, with barely enough speed to still fly, yet slow enough that we were able to ground loop near the end of our rollout, short of the buildings on each side of the street. We would have lost the wings if we hit them.

The return to our base involved transportation by Model A Ford trucks but mostly modern train travel to Bucharest, Rumania and a few days stay at a monastery, until being flown by C47 air force transport to Bari, Italy, from where we were again flown back to our base at Pantanella.

Irvin Eatman* invited me to talk about this for about fifteen minutes. Dale said fifteen to twenty minutes. I have hurriedly read this far for my wife to time for me. When I asked the time she said, "Only seven minutes and you didn't tell them about the screaming of the men with the broken legs when the mules they were riding went through the deep snow, nor about the trains you were supposed to be riding running out of water on the mountain, shoveling snow in the engine in lieu of water, then having to help push the train on up the mountain. Also, you said absolutely nothing about your experiences of the nine other days it took you to get back to your base, nor your disappointment at finding your tent and personal belongings gone when you did finally return. And what about that later time you were also shot up so badly you had to land behind Russian lines and your parents again received 'Missing in Action' notices, which you did not even mention the first time?"

* Curtis "Cy" Eatman was Irvin's father and Dale was Curtis's daughter. Betty Eatman was Curtis's wife. When Curtis passed away Charles "Chuck" Haynes married Betty!

www.ingramcontent.com/pod-product-compliance
Lightning Source LLC
LaVergne TN
LVHW041613070426
835507LV00008B/213